797

IMAGINING THE GOSPELS

IMAGINING THE GOSPELS

Kathy Galloway

illustrations by Graham Maule

TRIANGLE

First published in Great Britain 1988
First Triangle edition 1994
SPCK
Holy Trinity Church
Marylebone Road
London NW1 4DU

Copyright © Kathy Galloway 1988
Illustrations copyright © The Iona Community 1988

All rights reserved. No part of this book may be reproduced or transmitted in any form or by any means, electronic or mechanical, including photocopying, recording, or by any information storage and retrieval system, without permission in writing from the publisher.

British Library Cataloguing in Publication Data

Galloway, Kathy
 Imagining the Gospels
 1. Bible. N.T. Gospels. Critical studies
 I. Title
 226'.06

ISBN 0-281-04388-4

Printed in Great Britain by
BPC Paperbacks Ltd
Member of the British Printing Company Ltd

*For Janet, Jack, David, Lesley and Callum,
who rocked the cradle of my imagination,
with love.*

Acknowledgements

Thanks are due to Graham Maule of the Iona Community, whose illustrations so enliven the book, to my aunt, Agnes Cluness, for typing the manuscript, to the Resident Group at Iona Abbey for their encouragement and practical help, to Philip Law of SPCK for the invitation to write this book, and, especially, to my husband, Ian Galloway, for his many perceptive comments and suggestions on the manuscript and for his unfailing support and willingness to help me find the time to write in the midst of a very busy schedule.

All scriptural quotations are taken from the Good News Bible published by The Bible Societies and Collins, copyright © American Bible Society 1976.

The extract from 'Christ is alive' by Brian A. Wren (1936–) is reprinted by permission of Oxford University Press.

Contents

	Introduction	1
1	The Rich Man: 'Jesus looked at him with love.'	8
2	Jesus and Zacchaeus: 'Jesus was passing through . . .'	19
3	Jesus Heals Ten Men: 'Where are the other nine?'	27
4	The Lost Son: 'Everything I have is yours.'	37
5	The Pharisee and the Tax Collector: 'Not . . . like everybody else.'	46
6	The Killing of the Children: 'For they are all dead.'	54
7	Jesus Visits Martha and Mary: 'Martha was upset.'	61
8	The Woman Caught in Adultery: 'They all left, one by one, the older ones first.'	72
9	Jesus at the Home of Simon the Pharisee: 'Whoever has been forgiven little shows only a little love.'	85
10	Jesus is Anointed at Bethany: 'The sweet smell of the perfume filled the whole house.'	95
	Appendix: Imagining the Gospels as a Group Activity	103

Introduction

There is a folk hymn of the 1960s which begins, 'When Jesus came to our town . . .' I have imagined these familiar stories from the Gospels as if they happened in *my* town, my country, my world. I have shut myself in a room on my own, put a piece of blank paper in my typewriter, and, with the Bible open beside me, I have written them as they came to me, simply imagining them to be taking place now, in places I am familiar with, and among people I know.

The first time I ever did something like this was when I was fourteen years old. The National Bible Society was running a competition for schoolchildren to write an essay on a New Testament story, imagining that the writer was one of the characters in the drama. Everyone in our Religious Knowledge class was invited to enter. I don't remember how many did, but I wrote an account of the healing of the lame man at the Beautiful Gate in Jerusalem, found in the third chapter of the book of Acts. I wrote it imagining that I was Peter. To my surprise, I won second prize, a modest book-token, which interested me considerably more than how I had come by it. I did nothing like that again for many years.

In the intervening time, I read the Bible, studied theology, learned more about the historical background to the Old and New Testaments, and a lot about doctrine and dogma. As someone who does a lot of preaching, I grappled with texts and passages, trying to understand them in a way that I could share with others. Then a few years ago, I was invited to take part in a television series about house churches. In these, a group of people from different backgrounds and denominations were to spend six weeks doing Bible studies from Luke's gospel. Once a week we met in a studio, and our discussion was filmed. The person directing the programmes asked each of us to make one special commitment – to read the whole of Luke's Gospel straight through from beginning to end between every meeting. This we all agreed to do.

I thought I knew the New Testament pretty well. But reading it like this, as you would read a novel, six times in six weeks, was a revelation. The people in the tremendous story came alive for me in a completely new way. They assumed a reality they had never had when they were the material for study, the players in a drama of long ago. Though I believe my faith was real enough, and though I had a strong sense of Jesus as a living presence in my life, I had never before seen my life as relating so strongly to those of Zacchaeus, Mary and Martha, the disciples and all the other men and women whose lives were touched by Jesus. I began to have a much fuller understanding of the communion of saints as a dynamic force which transcends all barriers of time and place. From there, it was only a small step from trying to imagine the lives, thoughts, fears and hopes of men and women in the Palestine of two thousand years ago, and the impact Jesus had on them, to trying to picture the impact he would have coming to birth in Scotland in the world of the late twentieth century.

I found that for me, this had come to be an inevitable and necessary next step. When I tried to look back, there were so many limitations. I found that my imagination was limited by cultural and social differences. Try as I might, I just did not have the necessary knowledge of the kind that is based on experience, to understand enough about what it was like, how it might feel, to be a woman in Jewish society in the time of Jesus – what food I would have eaten, what clothes I would have worn, how I would have spent my spare time, who would have been the influences on my life. I find it very hard, for example, to imagine what it would be like not to be able to read. Having said this, I must also say that I recognize that these limitations are by no means universal, that there are many people and many societies living in the world today who could imagine these things much better than I can, because their own lives are lived in a very similar fashion – people who live in rural, pastoral economies, people who live under the heel of a foreign power, people whose government is one which does not have the separation of church and state, people in countries with high levels of illiteracy, women whose lives are

Introduction

circumscribed in a similar way to those whom Jesus knew. My way of life grants me many privileges, but it does effectively remove me from being able to identify with much of the way of life Jesus lived.

Secondly, I found that my capacity to imagine the way it was then was limited by two thousand years of ecclesiastical gloss, and by the mystique that attaches to 'Scripture'. So much has been hung on these stories, so many interpretations, doctrines, decisions, so many laws passed, so many wars fought, so many people killed, or saved, so many saints and heroes born from them, that it is sometimes hard to crawl from under the weight of history and look at them with new eyes. And it seems a little ironic that their status as the inspired Word of God (with which I would not disagree one bit) should sometimes serve to deter one's entry into the stories because the concern for how one is supposed to understand them prevents the discovery of how one actually *does* understand them.

And finally, I found that too often I was reading the stories through other eyes than my own. Other people's insights, other people's ideas, other people's imaginations, whether shared in preaching, writing, or late-night conversations, were valuable, helpful and inspiring. But they are not, and never can be, a substitute for a personal attempt to engage with the stories of the Gospels so that their meaning and intention might address my life, here and now.

And so, to imagine how it would affect me and the places and people around me if these events were taking place today, has been enormously helpful. I believe that through it, I have heard more clearly what the Word of God is saying to *me*. In that sense, as a kind of listening, it is a form of prayer.

The first story I imagined in this way was that of the Prodigal Son. I have always had a sneaking sympathy for the elder brother in that story, and, on reading something someone had written about the passage, I became so incensed on his behalf, and on behalf of all the people like him (but mainly me), that I sat down to try to imagine *his* story, and what Jesus was saying about and through him. I found my answer in the verse, 'everything I have is yours'.

From there, it all made sense to me. I experienced it as a moment of illumination.

That story is in this book. And you may not agree with my imagining of it one little bit. You may even find it offensive. But that's fine. I don't expect or hope for everyone to agree with me. (In fact, if my understanding does no more than make you think about the story again, I would be more than happy.) As I said, I am limited by who I am as much in imagining these stories happening now as I was in trying to imagine them in their historical setting. It's just that the limitations are different. Looking back, I was limited by not sharing the same environment and experience as them. Looking out into my own world, I am limited by not sharing the same environment and experience as you. The conditioning that shapes our understanding and imagination is particular and unique to each one of us. Where we live, what we believe, who influences us, and much more, will affect what we bring with us to each story, and it is that collection of experiences, prejudices, values and expectations contained in us that God will begin to dialogue with. So it is important that no one should take my imagining of the stories as in any way definitive, as suggesting that my interpretation is the right one. They are not a last word on anything. Even for me, they are barely a first word, more another step into the treasure-house of faith.

By the same token, the fact that we imagine and interpret through the screen of our own experience, culture and personality does not render our imagining invalid. All biblical interpretation has done exactly the same thing, and even the driest of biblical scholars cannot be detached from their context, as indeed the gospel writers themselves could not be. The fact that Luke was a Gentile shows as much in his account of Jesus' life as the fact of Matthew's Jewishness does in his. What matters is that we recognize our limitations for what they are, an acceptance of the fact that we can never achieve total understanding or lay down definitive rules about the Scriptures, and for what they are not, which is a prohibition on the way we may meet Jesus in the Scriptures. We all have to read the Gospels with our own particular and unique backgrounds and experience,

Introduction

but it is in and through this background and experience that we meet God, and there is no other way of meeting God than as who we are.

It is to share some of the fruits of my imagining, and to encourage others to think of doing this as an activity of faith that this book is offered. Many, many people, of course, already do this, and imaginative contemplation of the Gospels is a very ancient tradition in the Church. Ludolph of Saxony, a fourteenth-century Carthusian monk, wrote this about imagining the Gospels:

Hear and see these things being narrated, as though you were hearing with your own ears and seeing with your own eyes, for these things are most sweet to him who thinks on them with desire, and even more so to him who tastes them. And although many of these things are narrated as past events, you must meditate them all as though they were happening in the present moment; because in this way you will certainly taste a greater sweetness. Read then of what has been done as though they were happening now. Bring before your eyes past actions as though they were present. Then you will feel how full of wisdom and delight they are.

(From the Preface to *Vita Christi* by Ludolph of Saxony.)

The truth of his last sentence I can bear witness to.

And, as many people as there are who try this imaginative approach to the Gospels, so there are as many ways of actually doing it. I cannot lay down rules about method, nor would I want to. I have described my starting-point earlier in this chapter. Thereafter, I have included questions which I hope may encourage the imagination of others. I think that to do justice to the stories, it helps to give the imagination sufficient time to warm to the story, and to wander off on what are often valuable sidetracks. But you can do it anywhere, if you know the passage well – on the long bus journey home from work, for example, or while hanging out the washing.

If you can, try to give some outward expression to your imagining, simply because it helps to give form and clarity. Make notes, keep a diary, write it as a story or a poem, perhaps even paint or draw a picture of it. This kind of imagining can also be done equally helpfully in a group (see

Appendix, p. 103), and then the sharing of your thoughts with others can serve to focus your mind. Don't be afraid to use your senses, but see if you can imagine the sounds, the colours, the smells even, which would surround an event. But please don't try to force yourself into imagining if you find it uncomfortable or distressing. It's good when it comes naturally, and you can let your thoughts soar, but to do it when it doesn't feel comfortable may simply mean it's the wrong moment, or that there are other approaches to the Gospels which are more helpful for you. Your prayer is no less valid because this particular way doesn't suit you, just as praise is no less valid if it comes from the singing of hymns in a small church instead of from the Hallelujah Chorus sung by Westminster Abbey choir, or the plainsong chant of a monastery, or a rock gospel group.

And please don't think there is anything special about my imagination. There isn't. I have simply gained some knowledge about describing it on paper. We all have the ability to imagine at least a little, to ask ourselves the question 'what would it be like if Jesus came to my town?'. And in any case, the value of imagining the Gospels lies in the extent to which it helps us to meet Jesus in our own lives, and that does not at all depend for its success on the vividness of the imagination, only on our openness to listen and hear.

My own experience of imagining the Gospels has, as well as enriching me with the discovery that the Gospels offer an almost physical nourishment that is as real as the sacraments and the community of the Church, surprised me considerably. I find that I have never quite appreciated before how very subversive Jesus must have seemed to his contemporaries. The challenge that he presented to both religious and secular values and authority was not political in the same way as that offered by the various groups dedicated to the overthrow of Roman rule, but it was far more revolutionary. And I have found every story, even that of the killing of the children, holds the seeds of grace within it. It may be that this is because of the particular stories I have been moved to imagine, but I think not. I think these are in all the stories.

But more than this, even, I have found that imagining the Gospels is not just an aid to faith. It is also a call to action. In every story, I found the questions changing, as they moved from 'what would I do?' through 'what did I do?' to 'what must I do?' Jesus does not meet us to leave us where we are, but so that we can follow him into the future. A few years ago, a friend and fellow-member of the community I was then living in, hit the headlines, and even appeared on the television news, when he declared, in the context of a housing crisis in a run-down area of Edinburgh, 'Jesus Christ is alive and well and living in West Pilton'. The effect this statement had on people was the kind of effect the Gospels should have in the lives of those for whom they have been made real – excitement, curiosity, determination. It was news. In that situation, it was very definitely good news. It was saying, in actions as well as words, 'Jesus Christ is alive and well and living in West Pilton – so the least we can do is make sure that he and his neighbours have a decent place to live.'

I began by quoting from a modern folk hymn, and I want to end in the same way. In the end, what matters in imagining the Gospels is not just that we believe that we can authenticate the message of Christ by finding that these stories are real because they ring true to our experience. It is not just that in them, we may find a way to come closer to Jesus by allowing the people who spoke to him to speak to us. It is that we allow ourselves to be changed by Jesus, speaking to us now through the words of the past, and calling us to live the Gospels now, in *our* town, in *our* country, in *our* world. And Jesus will meet us anywhere we look for him, not only in the pages of the Bible, but in the pages of the newspaper, not only in the faces of Mary and Martha and Peter and Zacchaeus, but in the faces of the people who live in the same house, who work in the same office as us. Imagining the Gospels becomes most valid when it helps us to appreciate and act upon that belief.

> *Christ is alive! No longer bound*
> *by distant years in Palestine,*
> *but saving, healing, here and now,*
> *and touching every place and time.*
>   (from 'Christ is alive' by Brian Wren)

1. The Rich Man

'Jesus looked at him with love'
MARK 10.17–31

As Jesus was starting on his way again, a man ran up, knelt before him, and asked him, 'Good Teacher, what must I do to receive eternal life?'

'Why do you call me good?' Jesus asked him. 'No one is good except God alone. You know the commandments: "Do not commit murder; do not commit adultery; do not steal; do not accuse anyone falsely; do not cheat; respect your father and your mother."'

'Teacher,' the man said, 'ever since I was young, I have obeyed all these commandments.' Jesus looked straight at him with love and said, 'You need only one thing. Go and sell all you have and give the money to the poor, and you will have riches in heaven; then come and follow me.' When the man heard this, gloom spread over his face, and he went away sad, because he was very rich.

Jesus looked round at his disciples and said to them, 'How hard it will be for rich people to enter the Kingdom of God!' The disciples were shocked at these words, but Jesus went on to say, 'My children, how hard it is to enter the Kingdom of God! It is much harder for a rich person to enter the Kingdom of God than for a camel to go through the eye of a needle.' At this, the disciples were completely amazed and asked one another, 'Who, then, can be saved?'

Jesus looked straight at them and answered, 'This is impossible for man, but not for God; everything is possible for God.'

Then Peter spoke up, 'Look, we have left everything and followed you.'

'Yes,' Jesus said to them, 'and I tell you that anyone who leaves home or brothers or sisters or mother or father or children or fields for me and for the gospel, will receive much more in this present age. He will receive a hundred times more houses, brothers, sisters, mothers, children and fields — and persecutions as well; and in the age to come he will receive eternal life. But many who now are first will be last, and many who now are last will be first.'

It was not a fair thing to ask. Anyone in their right mind could see how unreasonable it was. To ask me to go and sell everything I own, and give the money to the poor. And then to join him and his followers. You can see what a ridiculous request it was.

I've tried all my life to be a good man. I've never been in trouble, never broken the law. I do my job honestly and to the best of my ability, I've always been considerate towards my parents, and I hope I'm a responsible citizen. I've always tried to live a good life, and I think the people who know me would tell you that I'm a good friend, who just wants to do what's kind and right. I don't *think* I'm boring or stuffy or pious—I have a sense of humour, and I know how to enjoy myself, without, I hope, hurting anyone else. Just an ordinary person, trying to do his best. That's why it does seem a little unfair that he should have asked that of me. After all, it's not as if I'd been a real reprobate, with a lot of debts to society to pay back.

I'm still not sure what made me speak to him. I don't usually do things that impulsively. I guess it was just that everything I've heard and seen of him seemed so attractive, as if he was the kind of person who could help you understand, make sense of things that were bothering you. I know he has a good reputation as a preacher and a counsellor, a lot of people seem to have been helped by him, although he's certainly unorthodox in his lifestyle. I suppose I thought he could help me with my faith, act as a sort of spiritual adviser.

Not that I've got a lot of problems really. Life's been good to me, and I suppose most people would think that I had it made. A very good job, even though I'm still quite young, a good education, a happy family life, and parents who've always tried to give me every advantage. I've never had to worry about money, and though I'm not one of those who goes in for conspicuous consumption, there's no doubt it is pleasant not to have to think about where your next meal's coming from, and whether you can scrape enough cash together for a new pair of shoes. I suppose I do have a very enviable life – not that I go around throwing my weight about, or thinking I'm any better than anyone else because I'm well off.

It's just that for a while now I've had this sense of something missing in my life. It's as if it's all slightly flat, lacking in sparkle, a little washed out. There's a kind of emptiness about it. I keep getting the feeling that there must be more to life, a secret that somehow evades me, is always just round the corner. Some days, I find myself driving home from work, or waking up in the morning, and asking myself, 'Is that it?' And I start to think about dying, and about someone trying to write my obituary, and what they would say about me, how my life would be judged. It's uncomfortable when you start thinking about the meaning of your life. I think I hoped that he might be able to help me understand what my life means.

You see, I knew that my problem wasn't a material one. For most people, it seems that worries and anxieties about the quality of their lives focus on much more ordinary things – they think life would be better if they could just get a better-paid job, or move to a different neighbourhood, or give their children more of the good things in life. Perhaps it's easier for poor people. When they've got worries about their lives, they can just assume that, if they had more money, everything would be much better. They can put their finger on the problem. But I couldn't. I *knew* that mine was not a social or financial problem. And so, by a process of elimination, I came to the conclusion that it was a spiritual one.

I suppose I'm quite a religious person. I was brought up in the church, and have stayed in it. I quite enjoy the services – I like singing, and there's something reassuring about Sundays going to church, a sense that here is something that is reliable, that doesn't change. It gives you the feeling that God's in his heaven and all's right with the world. And I give (pretty generously) to the church, and to a number of charities I've supported. I've even been to a few Bible studies, and quite liked them. But it still wasn't enough. That's why I asked the question.

If I think about it, I reckon that it was partly the sheer unexpectedness of his answer that made me feel unfairly treated, put on the spot. Of course, I was expecting to be asked about my life and principles, and so on. It was the other bit that was such a shock. I was really expecting something quite different. With a spiritual question, I expected a spiritual answer. I thought he might talk to me about praying a lot more, and maybe give me some guidelines on prayer to follow. Or a course of theological reading, or maybe even some spiritual exercises I could practise. I wouldn't have been altogether surprised if he'd suggested that I go and do some voluntary work, perhaps with some particularly unfortunate group of handicapped children, or even if he'd asked me if I felt a call to the ministry. But I certainly didn't expect that, when I asked a preacher about my spiritual life, he'd start talking about my money. I must confess that I was disappointed in him. I thought it displayed a lot of naivety, a lack of common sense. Put simply, it was a foolish answer.

Not that I think I couldn't do it. I dare say I could get used to wearing shabby clothes and eating in sleazy cafés. I could cope with walking everywhere, or travelling by public transport, and millions of people live in bad housing, so I suppose I could do it if I had to. But that's the point. I don't have to. Why make a virtue out of poverty, if you don't have to?

It's not as if it would make that much of a difference. I'm well off, yes, I grant you, but even the thousands I would raise by selling off my possessions would just be like a drop in the ocean; it would scarcely cause a ripple. It's a bad use of money. It would be much more sensible, for example, for me to set up a trust fund, which, carefully administered, could provide a nice little income for some worth-while project, or even help the preacher set himself up in a building somewhere, with a proper office where he could see people privately instead of in public on the street corner. Do some decent publicity, set up meetings, and so on. That would be much more sensible.

But what possible good would it do anyone to have me swelling the ranks of the unemployed? I don't have to be a burden on anyone at the moment, but I would be if I gave it all away. Besides, I've never had to take charity from anyone, and I wouldn't like to start.

I really could be much more use where I am. I have access to a lot of things that are really a necessity if any venture's going to succeed in today's world – a car, a telephone, newspapers and books. These things are not to be sneered at. It's not as if I use my money badly or irresponsibly. I don't buy flashy jewellery, or take cruises in the sun. I don't hold riotous parties, or waste my money on a lot of executive toys. But obviously it makes good economic sense to buy good-quality things because they last far better. It's sensible to take a decent holiday, even if it's just a couple of weeks in the country fishing, because then you work much more efficiently the rest of the time. And (not that I'm contemplating marriage just now), you couldn't possibly expect a woman to take on that kind of insecurity, and you'd never be able to have children if you didn't do your best to make sure they had a decent way of life. I really do get irritated with that kind of sloppy thinking. It's the way of the world that a lot of the most worth-while things cost money. If you left it to people like him, you wouldn't have wonderful things like symphony orchestras, because no one would be able to afford music lessons for their children. You'd have no artistic life, no cultural life. We'd all be

The Rich Man

ground down to some lowest common denominator existence. I've seen what poverty can do to people, and it's not romantic, it doesn't make them any nobler or better. Mostly it just makes people violent and brutish and greedy.

Where I am just now, I'm respected, I have access to where the power is. I'd lose all that if I threw my money away and started behaving like some kind of drop-out. Wouldn't it be much better, given the fact that money means power, to have that money working for you, to have the power on your side? And anyway, it's out of the question because of what it would do to my parents. It would distress them terribly – in fact, it might well give my father a heart attack. It would be quite unfair to them after all they've done for me. And my friends would all think I'd taken leave of my senses. They *really* would lose all respect for me. I don't even know how I'd feel about myself. It would go so much against the grain, it would be against everything I've learned and believed. Could I really do something which would be so unnatural?

I was pretty depressed, then. I'd gone looking for spiritual answers, and instead had it suggested to me that I might give away all my money and join this man in his wanderings. As I said, not what I expected at all. Not a realistic proposition. And yet, I still don't feel right about it. Not just about being put on the spot in that very public way, in front of that odd collection of hangers-on, but about him. I really felt that he might have been able to help me. The way he looked at me then, I can't describe it, but it was as if he looked right into me and saw me, as I was, and yet as I wasn't too. As if he saw something wonderful and exciting in me. I couldn't help liking him, even when he was saying these ridiculous things. Perhaps he could have come home with me, we could have talked. But he didn't suggest it.

If only life were simpler. It must be so much easier for people who don't have to be sensible, don't have to make choices, don't have to be responsible for others. How lovely just to be able to throw caution to the winds, and go. But, as I said, that's simply not realistic. And here I am, still with my spiritual problem. If only he'd said something that could have answered that.

*   *   *

You had to feel sorry for the poor guy, in front of everyone, having to turn and go away with his tail between his legs. Not that *I'm* a great one for feeling much sympathy for the rich and famous, but you could see that he was at least genuine. You could tell that old J.C. liked him, too, and he looked really disappointed when he went away with his face tripping him. But what could you expect? Asking a guy like that to give everything away and follow him round the country.

Of course, we've all done that too. But it's not that hard to give up everything when you haven't got that much to lose in the first place. At least in terms of hard cash. We did have to get used to the idea that not only were we not rich now, but it was extremely unlikely that we were ever going to be so, J.C. being the kind of person who doesn't seem to go down too well with those and such-as-those. And I suppose that was harder than we thought it might be, watching that particular castle in the air come tumbling down. Apart from being the things that everyone encourages you to do, right from your childhood – get on, get out, get up – it's also the dream that gets you through a lot of long nights, a lot of hard times. Many's the time the wife and me have sat beside the fire talking about what we'd do with the money when our number came up, when our ship came home. (We knew it'd have to be some stroke of luck like that – folk like us never get anywhere near actually *making* the big money.) Times when the fishing was very poor, and we didn't know whether we'd make it through to the end of the week, or when one of the kids was sick, and we couldn't take them away for a holiday, times when the wife's mother's nagging was just too much, and we would have done anything for a bigger house so there was a room where we could go just to get out of earshot for an hour. To be honest, I still don't think the wife's come to terms with it completely. And it is more work for her, with me being away so much, and her never quite sure where I am, and what kind of trouble we'll end up in next. But she understands why I'm doing it, and she believes in him too. In fact, she'll not hear a word against him, ever since her mother recovered from that illness when he was there, and she swears it was him who healed her. And the one thing

The Rich Man

that stops me worrying more about her and the kids is knowing that we've got good friends. I know a lot of them don't approve, or even understand what I'm doing, but they'll still help out, they'll not see her short. Tell you the truth, I think, if it's possible, she'd actually like to be with me. Maybe the next time...

But that's by the way. As I was saying, it maybe wasn't so hard for us, who didn't have much to lose – and anyway, there's that much going on all the time that you've no time for daydreams, never knowing what's going to happen next, or who you're going to meet. But to ask a young fellow like that, with all his money, to just give it away! You could see the young fellow didn't like it, and who can blame him? See, with them, it's not just the money, it's everything that goes with it. The status, the respect of the community, a high place in the church. That's a man who's been used to being his own boss, to making his own decisions, to being in control of things. That's an awful lot of power to give up, and for what? To go roaming round the country with a wandering preacher who half the folk think is a new Messiah, and the other half think is a dangerous lunatic, or worse, a dangerous communist. Can you see a fellow like that, with his expensive education, going around with a crowd like us, always just one step ahead of the authorities (so far), putting up with our daft questions, or even more, putting up with the not-always-too-gentle raps on the knuckles we get from J.C. when we're particularly dense. I don't see it. Not at all. People like that want to have everything cut and dried, they like to know exactly what's what and who's who. He wouldn't like being a nobody. He wants to be in charge of his own life.

That's another thing we've never got used to. When you're not very educated, not very well off, not very important, there's plenty of folk to tell you what to do, where to go, how to live your life. That's one of the things I liked about J.C. He let us make our own decisions, didn't try to make them for us. First of all, he did us the honour of choosing us (though God knows why, 'cause I don't). Then he simply waited for us to decide, like we really were people whose decisions counted. But that was a hard choice he gave that young fellow, and you can't blame him for choosing the way he did. I don't know if I'd have done differently in his shoes. Of course, Matthew did it, gave away his money, I mean. But that was different. He was a crook. It wasn't his money anyway. But you could tell the young fellow was a *very* respectable person. That's why it was such a shock when J.C. started going on about the rich having a hard job getting into the Kingdom. Well, of course, Matthew we could understand that about, he had stolen and cheated and lied, and you wouldn't welcome him many places. But the young fellow was not like that at all. He was your typical, honest, upright type, churchgoing and all that. The kind you think God must really like for him to have so much going for him. If he couldn't get in, what hope was there for the rest of us ordinary folk who're always making mistakes and putting our foot in it. I'm still trying to work out why he shouldn't get in, and the only thing I can see is to do with the thing about following J.C., which is obviously important, since I'm definitely of the opinion that he's been sent by God. The young fellow really was genuine, and probably did want to follow him, but something was even more important to him. It got in his way. Whether it was the money, or the status or the power, I don't know. Perhaps it was just liking to be his own master. Because obviously, you couldn't follow J.C. and still be your own boss. It's quite clear that we're following him. We're the learners. The only thing that we've got going for us is that we're here. The young fellow had a lot going for him, too much for him to be here too. It's just as well it's up to God and not us, because these things are pretty confusing to my mind.

So that's what I said, then, that at least we're here, and maybe there's some hope for us. Then J.C. started talking in riddles again, saying that whatever we'd left behind, we'd get a hundred times as much from life, and persecution as well. Well, that bit I can quite understand. We're certainly getting used to not being the most popular folk around, and if I think about it much (which I try not to do most of the time, because it frightens me), I can see us heading for disaster. But the hundred times as much is not so clear. In fact, it's not clear at all. We're poorer than when we started, we never know whether there's going to be a bed for us, and most of us have left our families behind. Right enough, we've had quite a lot of very nice hospitality along the way. And it is true that we've met folk who've opened their homes to us as if we were their long-lost relatives. I reckon we've made friendships that'll last a lifetime. And these guys with me – well, we don't always see eye to eye about everything, but we've certainly been through experiences which have brought us very close together. I guess they are really like brothers. I wonder if that's what he meant?

Well, the young fellow went off looking pretty gloomy. As I said, I did feel sorry for him, because in spite of everything, I wouldn't be anywhere else. I know that it's far from a quiet life, but there's a real sense of adventure, a real feeling that you're learning new things all the time. I feel my life's got some point to it, and that does give a bit of sparkle to life. It makes the sky seem more blue somehow. I don't know what I've done to deserve it, and I wouldn't swop it for that fellow's money. God must love me right enough. Well, that's the rich for you. He's got a lot, but he wants it all, that young fellow. Must have been a bit of a shock for him to discover there are some things you can't buy. What J.C. offers, you can't buy that, otherwise I wouldn't be here. Funny, I never ever thought of money as being something that could get in your way, more as something that could let you get your way. As I said, I'm always learning. I wonder if the young fellow'll get home and wish he could change his mind? That'd be a real turn-up for the books. Oh well, I don't suppose we'll ever know . . .

*   *   *

Once again, Jesus is turning the received wisdom of his society on its head. The prevalent opinion among the Jews was that riches, or prosperity generally, were a sign of God's favour and approval. Once again, Jesus emphasizes that salvation cannot be bought, by wealth, good conduct, right living, or anything else. It is a gift of God's grace. Material wealth is an insidious snare, and many of us who judge the rich young man in the story are speaking from positions where we do not really understand the attractions of escape from bitter, grinding poverty. But even if money is not the thing which binds us, we all have our own particular dear thing which tempts us to the idolatry from which Jesus was offering to free the young man. And to him, though he would not compromise on what he demanded, Jesus was still kind, for he loved him.

Some questions to help your own imagining of this story:

1 What particularly strikes you about this story?
2 How does it make you feel about your possessions?
3 What would you say you are rich in?
4 What are the things that get in *your* way when you try to follow Jesus?

A story which points out some of the other things which can prevent us from following Jesus is the passage about the would-be followers of Jesus in Luke 9.57–62. What do you imagine in it are the things that bind us, and where do you see that in your own life? Or read the story of the widow's offering in Mark 12.41–4, and imagine what it would mean for you to do as she did.

2. Jesus and Zacchaeus

'Jesus was passing through'
LUKE 19.1–10

Jesus went on into Jericho and was passing through. There was a chief tax collector there named Zacchaeus, who was rich. He was trying to see who Jesus was, but he was a little man and could not see Jesus because of the crowd. So he ran ahead of the crowd and climbed a sycamore tree to see Jesus, who was going to pass that way. When Jesus came to that place, he looked up and said to Zacchaeus, 'Hurry down, Zacchaeus, because I must stay in your house today.'

Zacchaeus hurried down and welcomed him with great joy. All the people who saw it started grumbling. 'This man has gone as a guest to the home of a sinner!'

Zacchaeus stood up and said to the Lord, 'Listen, sir! I will give half my belongings to the poor, and if I have cheated anyone, I will pay him back four times as much.'

Jesus said to him, 'Salvation has come to this house today, for this man, also, is a descendant of Abraham. The Son of Man came to seek and to save the lost.'

'Donald! Can you get the door . . . ?'

'Is that you, Jean? Just go into the living-room, I'll be down in a minute, I'm just changing my shoes.

'D'ye fancy going up the town, have a wee wander round the shops. It's a lovely day, we could see if there's a show on in the gardens, and maybe go and have our tea somewhere? Aye, I know it'll be busy, but we could always take a taxi back, and not have to wait for buses. Anyway, I've got that dress to take back to the shop, you know, the blue one that was too tight across the shoulders. I thought I might see if it would fit better in the next size. If we hurry now, we'll just catch the bus at ten-past-two . . .

'Good grief, it's busy, isn't it? It's not usually this busy on a Tuesday. D'ye think there's something special on? I don't remember reading anything in the paper about anything special happening today. It's next week, isn't it, that the Princess is coming to open that new centre. And there can't be a match on on a Tuesday. Donald never said anything about a match today, and he'd know if anyone would, he never misses a game! Maybe it's the gala day somewhere, there seems to be an awful lot of people in town today. I hope we don't have to wait in too long a queue to change that dress. Here, let's get over the road while the lights are at red . . .

'Oh, my feet are killing me! It's hot, isn't it? That shop was like a sardine-tin, and what about that woman giving me all the cheek about not having a receipt for the dress. Stuck-up besom! "I'm sorry, Madam, but how do we know you bought the dress in this branch?" I'll "Madam" her! D'ye fancy going and getting a cup of tea now? There's that nice wee place away along at the other end of the street. They do very nice chocolate eclairs. We could cross over and walk along to it through the gardens. It'll be a lot quieter there, and it's nice and cool with all the trees. We could even have a wee seat and watch the pigeons for a bit. Right? . . .

Jesus and Zacchaeus   21

'There must be something on! Look at all these folk along there, and they're all standing about. They look as if they're waiting for something. Or someone. Maybe there's going to be a show in the bandstand. Country dancing or something! Aye, I know there's never anybody watches the country dancing except the tourists, but what can it be? Well anyway, I'm not going back over that road again, it's just as busy on the other side and, anyway, maybe it's quieter further along. We'll just need to fight our way through . . .

'Hey, you, sonny. Watch who you're shoving! I tell you, Jean, young people nowadays, they've no respect for the older generation. When we were young, you would never dream of pushing older folk like that, and never even saying sorry. I don't know why all these young folk are here hanging about, they should be at work, or in the school. See all this unemployment, it's not right, kids hanging about all day, and getting cheeky with their elders. Mind you, there's quite a few men here as well, oh, and there's Mrs Jackson that's your Jimmy's mother-in-law's next door neighbour over there, no, not there, away over there, right at the front of the crowd. What d'ye think's going on, Jean, d'ye think it's one of these demonstrations? No, it couldn't be that, you'd never find Mrs Jackson on one of them, she thinks they should all be locked up. Here, let's try and get over beside her, and see if she knows what's going on, she'll maybe know. If something's going to happen, we might as well get a grandstand view. Come on, just use your elbows a bit. We've no been going to the sales for years for nothing. Now, just hold on to me, and don't get lost. Just head for that big tree over there . . .

'It's no use! I can't get any further, I'm wedged in, and there's a wee laddie standing on my toe. Get off my feet, you! We'll just have to wait here till it's all over, whatever it is. I doubt we could even get back the way we came. I hope whoever it is is due soon. Here, Jeanie, look over there, at that big tree. There's even someone up the tree. Daft idiot, he doesn't look young enough to be playing about climbing trees. He'd better watch out or he'll be falling out and breaking his leg, aye, and maybe hurting folk standing under the tree, there's a big press of folk over there. Would you believe it, Jeanie, I know that man! D'ye see, it's yon wee fellow that comes round to collect the club money down our way. He's a bad man, that one. Everyone knows him, he's aye there when you don't want him, turning up like a bad penny and giving decent folk a hard time. One of those wee men that likes to act big and throw his weight around, like he knows he's nothing and has to act important to cover it up. I bet he's feared inside, you can always tell when folk are feared, that's when they start turning the screws on people. *And* he's a swindler as well. I'm sure those interest rates he charges aren't right, he must be pocketing a fair whack of it himself. There's a lot of folk down our way have got themselves into real trouble through him – remember that nice young couple that used to live at number 7? Oh, he was hard on them, and even when the young chap lost his job, he still wanted his payments on the nail, never let up, he didn't. They had to give up their house and go back and live with her mother, they got into such debt. And I hear that there's problems with the marriage now, not surprising with all of them crammed into that wee house. I blame him for it, he could've given them a chance! And I heard that when he doesn't get his money, he's got some boys that come and make threats. It's not right, especially if there's children in the house.

'But he's smart, that one. No one can prove anything against him, and they're afraid to report him anyway. He's got big men behind him, he's just doing their dirty work for them. Aye, the world's ill-divided, isn't it, ordinary folk just trying to get on as best they can, getting taken in by folk with power, and they get away with it. There's no justice – not when you see a wee crook like that driving around in a fancy car, and wearing all that gold jewellery, watches and rings, the lot. I can't abide seeing a man wearing jewellery, it's not manly, is it? I bet he doesn't live in a council house, I bet he's got a big house somewhere on the outskirts of town. Oh, a nasty, sleazy wee man, that one. Nobody likes him, I wonder how he sleeps at night!

'What d'ye think he's doing up that tree at his age, playing the fool? Just nosey, I expect. That one doesn't like anything going on he doesn't know about. Here, Jean, something's happening, there's someone coming. Can you

Jesus and Zacchaeus 23

see anything back there? Hang on and I'll try and see if I can see who it is. Must be one of these pop singers or someone famous. Here he's coming now, he looks as if he's in a hurry, he's fairly striding along. I don't recognize him. Oh yes I do. Here, Jeanie, it's that fellow Sally was telling us about, some religious man, a preacher or something. Mind your Jimmy had some mates at work who heard him talking somewhere. No, no, he's not one of the ones that's always here on a Sunday ranting on about religion and the end of the world. No, he's not one of the Lodge ones, this is a new one. I don't think he's a minister, I heard that they were all up in arms about him, think he's bringing the church into disrepute or something. No, I heard he's just an ordinary fellow, comes from somewhere up north, used to be a joiner or something. Gave up his job to go around preaching, says he's been sent by God. Well, these days, you'd have to believe something like that to give up a good trade. Either that, or some kind of religious fanatic. But Jimmy was saying that his workmates were very impressed by him, he wasn't the usual kind of holier-than-thou preacher, going on about how everything you like doing's against the rules of the church. They said a lot of what he said made sense, *and* he talked like a human being, not all these "thees and thous" and big words. Well, it's about time somebody said things that make sense, not like the politicians, you can't trust them as far as you can throw them. Anyone that could make people a bit more thoughtful for each other, a bit less full of their own importance is worth a fair hearing before we all kill each other, *I think*. There's that many people around who wouldn't lift a finger to help you if you were dying by the side of the road. And too many who think they're God, and can just do what they like with ordinary folk. No wonder the young folk get into trouble, with the example they're set. But Sally says that this man's got some funny friends, right enough, not very respectable. Oh well, you can't judge till you know what you're judging, eh? I wonder if he's going to preach today – no it doesn't look like it, he's not stopping. Yes he is, can you see him, Jean, he's stopped just over there under the big tree. Oh, he's quite young, he's got a nice face, nice eyes, he's smiling . . . You'll never believe this, Jeanie, he's smiling up at that wee crook up the tree, he's talking to him. I don't know what he's wasting his breath on him for, you can tell what he's like just by looking at him. He's telling him to come down, Jeanie, he's telling him he's coming to stay the night with him. What about that, Jeanie, a wee swindler like him – oh, there's a lot of folk here know him, they're not liking that at all, they're shouting at him. I hope this isn't going to turn nasty. I don't think much of a preacher that goes around inviting himself to stay with wicked folk like that, doesn't say much for his judgement. He must be either a chancer himself or soft in the head.

'He's coming down out the tree. He doesn't half look daft, climbing down like a wee monkey. He's looking very pleased with himself, I must say. He's shaking his hand – what did Sally say the fellow's name was again? He's all over him. Here, he's saying something now, quiet while I see if I can hear him. He's standing up now, but he's that wee I can hardly see him.

'Well, Jeanie, would you believe it? D'ye know what the wee man's just said? I've never heard anything like it in my life. He says that he's going to pay back all the folk he's cheated *four times* what he cheated them out of. That'll cost him a pretty penny! And now he's saying that he's going to give half of everything he owns to charity. That's a man who never gave away a smile in his life! That young fellow must be some kind of miracle-worker. Fancy him saying that in front of all these folk. He'll not be able to get out of that so easily with so many witnesses. What if he means it? He'll need to sell his big car. Here, the young fellow's saying something else. Are you still there, Jean?

'He's saying that we're all human beings, and the wee man deserves a chance as much as anyone else. He's saying that he came to look for people who're lost!

'Well! What would you make of that? I wonder what he means, lost. Maybe he means folk who've lost their place in life. The wee man certainly can't have had much going for him for all his money. I certainly wouldn't like to work for *his* bosses. Not much fun to work for folk you couldn't turn your back on in case they stabbed you in it. Maybe that's what he meant. What do you think, Jeanie? Do you think he meant that you're lost if you can't look at yourself in the

Jesus and Zacchaeus 25

mirror in the morning? That's them away now. They're certainly looking pretty friendly. I wonder why the young fellow stopped like that. He looked as if he was just passing through. What d'ye think made him stop, Jeanie?

'Well, I hope he sticks to what he said. There'll be a lot of relieved folk around down our way if he does. But it's taking an awfully big risk, don't you think, Jeanie? To change like that, I mean, when you've always done things a certain way. Takes a lot of courage, especially if you do it in public. I like to see someone with that kind of courage. After all, if you don't take the chances in life when you get them, you might spend your whole life regretting it. Nothing ventured, nothing gained, that's what I always say. I hope folks don't give him a hard time, though. People can be cruel, and there'll be a lot who won't believe it till they see it. Always like to believe the worst about everyone. Och well, though, maybe if that young fellow's taken a liking to him, he'll be all right. Friends can get you through a lot of hard times, eh, Jeanie? He obviously sees something in him we missed. Who knows, maybe there's a lot more to come from the wee man. After this, nothing would surprise me. I'd like to see that young fellow again. Maybe he'd have a better way of explaining God than we're used to. Look, the crowd's thinning out now. We could get along for our tea, I could fair go a nice cup after all that excitement, and get the weight off my feet . . .

'You know something, Jean? It's nice to see somebody change like that. It gives you hope for the human race. There might even be hope for you and me, Jeanie, if someone like the wee man can do it. What d'ye think, hen? D'ye think the young fellow'd like to come and have tea with us? Maybe we'll ask him if we see him. Here, look at the time. We'd better get on our way. We've got a lot to do - a lot of folk to give the good news to down our way. Let's go. . .

'Taxi! . . .'

* * *

This is one of my favourite stories in the whole of the Bible. It is so full of grace, not just in the transformation which Jesus made possible for Zacchaeus, but in the way he offered it. It seems from the text that Jesus was not intending to stop at that place, he was just passing through. But in spite of the pressures on him, the crowds following him, and the momentum gathering around him, he had the freedom of decision which allowed him to change his plans and respond to Zacchaeus. And the delightful way in which he called to Zacchaeus, not berating him for his undeniable sin, but gently insistent that there was something Zacchaeus could do for *him*, gave Zacchaeus an opportunity to respond in a way that a lecture on his wrongdoing never could have done. Jesus reaching out in love, and speaking the words of personal acceptance, allowed the sinner the grace of repentance and transformation of life.

Some questions to help your own imagining of this story:

1. How do *you* visualize this scene?
2. How do you imagine Zacchaeus felt when Jesus called him down from the tree?
3. Have *you* ever felt left out, and then been included?
4. Where, today, do you see those who are excluded being brought in?
5. Who needs you to let them in, so that change can happen?

Jesus himself experienced the pain of rejection. Read the passage in Mark 6.1–6, where Jesus is rejected in his own home town of Nazareth. Try to imagine the scene if it was someone from *your* town, preaching in *your* local church. How would people react? How would you react?

3. Jesus Heals Ten Men

'Where are the other nine?'
LUKE 17.11-19

As Jesus made his way to Jerusalem, he went along the border between Samaria and Galilee. He was going into a village when he was met by ten men suffering from a dreaded skin disease. They stood at a distance and shouted, 'Jesus! Master! Take pity on us!'

Jesus saw them and said to them, 'Go and let the priests examine you.'

On the way they were made clean.

When one of them saw that he was healed, he came back, praising God in a loud voice. He threw himself to the ground at Jesus' feet and thanked him. The man was a Samaritan. Jesus said, 'There were ten men who were healed; where are the other nine? Why is this foreigner the only one who came back to give thanks to

God?' And Jesus said to him, 'Get up and go; your faith has made you well.'

I still can't believe it. Every morning when I wake up, the first thing I do is run my hands along my arms and legs, feeling for the pain, feeling for the numbness, searching anxiously for the ugly red blotches. And when, O thank God, when they're not there, I relive the moment it happened all over again. And the sun seems so blessedly warm, and the sky so blue that life seems the most miraculous thing that you could imagine. Then I get out of bed, and I breathe. I breathe right down to the bottom of my lungs, I fill them as if they are a big red balloon which a child is blowing up, and it goes on and on growing and growing until the child decides to tie it, and let it go floating off up into the sky. And I breathe out and my breath goes floating off into the sky, and my breath, deep and effortless, becomes a symbol of joy, like a child's balloon liberated to go where it wants, to drift into the unknown, carried by the breeze, and celebrating, celebrating, that life is good, and God is good.

Breathing has become so important to me. For so long, every breath I took was agony, even before it started to get difficult to breathe, and the smallest action would leave me gasping and weak and breathless. It began when the doctors told me the results of the tests. At that moment, a band of iron settled round my chest, and it never left me again until I met him. Back then, it was not my body that suffered. That came later. It was my spirit that could not breathe. The iron band that snapped shut around my breathing was a great sadness that imprisoned my spirit. Oh, there was fear, yes. I had seen what happened to other people when the world discovered their secret. And there was anger, that this should have happened to me. And there was a sense of loss at the thought of all the things I would never live to do and discover. But mostly there was just this terrible, nameless sadness for the sorrow of it all which wrapped itself round me, and clung, and would not let go.

I remember I started to cry, not loudly or dramatically, just tears dripping down my cheeks, a little flood of them, falling and falling, and they didn't know what to do. I got

Jesus Heals Ten Men

the impression that they might have been able to handle it better if I had shouted or sworn. As it was, they muttered sympathetic, embarrassed words. But no one touched me. Already there was a distance between them and me. Already, I had become untouchable. One minute you belong to the human race, the next you are something else, for ever alien. This was what it would be like – cast out for the rest of life. Of course, being an outsider was something I already had plenty of experience of. This is not an easy country in which to be a foreigner. Not that there's all that much outright racism or persecution, like there is in some places. The authorities will reluctantly step in if the nastiness gets too blatant. After all, it is in the law, that it's wrong to be unjust to foreigners, that you have to give them their rights, what rights are allowed them. But it's so easy for those in power to undermine the law, to damn it with faint praise, to dismiss it as the pious idealism of do-gooders, to act as if they are surprised and horrified by its most flagrant violations, when they have comfortably ignored every breach of its intention. People know when their leaders really believe in their law, and the people in this country take their lead from their leaders. So you get accustomed to a thousand subtle ways of making you feel inferior, an outsider. You get used to people telling their children that your children are dirty, and they mustn't play with them. You get used to hearing that your religion is inferior, superstitious, and that God intends you all for damnation. You get used to a way of life which in every detail is meant to show you that your culture, your food, your leaders, your ways, are second rate, and that the only hope for you is to become as much like them as possible. And having done their best to show you that, and to make your children ashamed of their parents, they then say, 'But of course, you can never really be one of us.' What refinement of cruelty. To say in one breath that your only salvation lies in becoming like them, and in the next breath to say that you can never hope to do that. Sometimes I have thought that beatings and imprisonment would be preferable. Oh yes, I was used to being an outsider already. I knew what it was like to be despised.

But this was different. Even a foreigner has things he can

cling to. He has his memories, he has his racial pride, he has his companions in anger. I had friends, I had plans, I had a vision of the time when things would be better for our people. I had a family. But this disease, this stigma that I was marked with now, this made me completely alone. From now on, I was anathema, shut out from the whole race of men. I knew that my people, even my family, would not accept me now. They are ordinary people, mostly concerned with making a living, with their prospects, with who is getting married and who is being born. Even if they could not bring themselves to believe what the priests said, that I was cursed, punished by God, they could not cope with all that this disease implied. To be shunned by their neighbours, to be pointed at in the street, to overhear the whispers, 'You know what's wrong with their son, don't you?', to watch me wither and waste away, and worry about which of their children might catch it next – it was more than they could face!

A knowledge came to me then, which everything that happened later confirmed, that the fear and ignorance and determination to hold on to what you have, which allows injustice and persecution to grow and run rampant, is not confined to one particular race or nationality or religion or class. It is not even confined to those who have power. The seeds of prejudice are everywhere, even in your own family. I knew that what had been done to them, my people would now be unable to resist doing to me. I guess that the iron band of sadness that imprisoned me came from this knowledge as much as from everything else.

After I learned the truth, everything happened exactly as I expected it would. My family rejected me. The church castigated me. My people cast me out. And I found myself in a strange new community – the community of the despised. There was nowhere else to go, and no one else to turn to. At first, in this strange new community, we were wary of each other. Old animosities die hard, and we watched one another suspiciously, one minute eager to see signs of improvement in another, because then there might be hope for us; the next minute filled with jealousy if another seemed better because it was not us. But gradually, the antagonism disappeared. There seemed so little point in it.

Jesus Heals Ten Men

After all, we were capable of no threat to anyone. And anyway, all of us had the mark of death on us. So we began to share our fears a little, and to take some comfort in the silence that often fell upon us, which was the silence of a common suffering. The world passed us by, and all but a few people avoided us. There were a few who gave us some material help, whether from guilt or fear was sometimes not clear. And there were a very few who gave us more than that. It was only them, and a kind of native stubbornness that stopped me from cursing God and taking a knife to my throat.

Because for a long time bitterness consumed me. Bitterness against my family, my friends, against life, against God. Or at least, against the God the clergy ranted of. Their God screamed at me that I deserved to die, that I was being punished for my sins. Well, I know I have not always been a good person. I have done my share of lying and cheating. I too have used others for my own ends, and harboured grudges. I may have been as bad as they said, though God knows, I didn't mean to hurt people. I just didn't know how to be the person I was without hurting. But I have seen the children, born with the stigma, helpless and unloved, I know that what awaits them is a few years of lonely pain, with little of the joy and hope and freedom of childhood. I have seen the ones who, blameless, caught the disease from a loved one. What are they being punished for? Is it for the offence of having been born? The God the clergy speak of is a monster. I, the loathsome and untouchable, wearing the marks of my sin on my flesh for all to see, would not punish these. Is God more vindictive than I, who have so much justification for bitterness? I want to ask these priests, these public pietists, where are the marks of sin on the flesh of those who let children starve while the rich grow fatter, who took a life in a stupor of drunkenness, who thought it was manly to beat up a woman, who trade in the commodities of human misery, who think freedom lies in possessions and not in a breath that can soar like a balloon carried by the breeze. Why, O God of the priests, does their skin remain smooth and unmarked? That God, I hated.

So I was bitter, so I believed that all that was left was the inexorable slide down into death. Everything fixed and final, no hope for a foreigner, a sinner. Only a God who damned me!

But then I met a man who changed everything, who made me believe once again that change was possible. This man saved my life, and set my spirit free. We were out one day for a walk, some of us, not coming from anywhere in particular, not going anywhere in particular, keeping well out of the way of the people in the village, who had not wanted us there, and resented our presence deeply. And we saw this man coming. We had heard about him, heard that he was a preacher, that he spent a lot of time with the lower elements in society, that the church disapproved of him strongly, and the politicians even more. We had heard that he was a healer. Now, when you've got something like we had, you tend to be rather sceptical of people claiming miracle cures, and to suspect that they're after something, money or power, or whatever. We had had our hopes raised so often. But on the other hand, we knew that the doctors could do nothing for us now, and maybe not for a long time (when it would be too late for us).

Perhaps there was also the sense that someone who was a kind of outsider himself would not shrink from the human contact we all craved. Anyhow, we started to shout to him, from where we were standing, and a pathetic lot we must have looked.

He came towards us, just an ordinary-looking man, quite young, and looked at us, and then he said the most extraordinary thing. He said, 'Go to the church, and let the priests look at you'. That was all he said, and then he just stood there. We looked at each other for a minute. What he asked was the most outrageous thing. People in the church generally were so unsympathetic that almost all of us had suffered from their attitude. And the clergy in the church in this village had led a campaign to prevent our house from being sited there, had said that it was an undesirable location, and that we'd be a danger to public health and morals, and would bring disreputable elements around. To ask us to go and see them was like asking us to go and put our heads in the lion's mouth.

But there was something about him, he had a kind of authority that made you want to do what he said. Perhaps it

Jesus Heals Ten Men

was the very unlikeliness of what he suggested that made us do it. It certainly didn't seem like he meant us any harm. So we started to walk towards the village, slowly at first, and then more confidently. We hadn't gone very far, when an extraordinary sensation of something which I can only describe as well-being suddenly started to move over me. I know it sounds crazy and quite irrational, but I can't think of any other way to describe it. I felt well. The weakness had gone from my arms and legs, and the blotches on my skin were fading. For a moment, I panicked. I thought, this is it, I'm going to die. The breath left me, and for a second I stood quite still, my mind clear of everything, all sound fading into the distance, looking inward into myself. I became quite calm. Then I looked up at the sky, and took a deep breath. As I breathed in, I nerved myself instinctively to feel the iron band round my chest. But it was not there. It was gone. I breathed, and breathed again. I felt as if I could go on inhaling for ever. And as I breathed out, I felt my spirit well up within me, and soar up into the sky. I felt free! I was free! It was such a magical thing. I turned, and started to run back to where the man was standing. I was shouting at the top of my voice, thank you God, thank you God. I fell to the ground beside him, and I could feel the warmth of the earth, and smell the grass. I don't know whether I was laughing or crying, but I thanked him over and over again. I looked up, and I saw that he was laughing too, and there were tears in his eyes. He bent down, and helped me to get up, and put his arm round my shoulder, and hugged me. I cried on his shoulder then.

Then he looked towards the village. I looked too, and saw that there was no sign of the others. I assumed that the same thing had happened to them, and that they had raced right into the village in their excitement. He turned to me, and there was sadness in his smile. 'There were ten of you', he said, 'What's happened to the others? Why is it that you, a foreigner, are the only one who's come back, the only one who wanted to say thank you to God? These others are *my* people, where are they?' Then the sadness left him, and he said, 'On you go, then. It's your own faith that's made you well.' Then he squeezed my hand, and walked off.

I stood for a long time watching him go, trying to

understand what had happened to me. My illness had given me a lot of knowledge about people, about their fears and prejudices, about their weakness and anger. But I had no way to use my knowledge, and so it had made me bitter. Now someone had shown me a way to use what I knew. This man, this healer, had knowledge. But he had courage and love as well. He had given us his love by coming close to us. And he had given us his courage to go and face the priests. That courage and love had touched in me what I did not know I had left – my last reserves of faith, faith in goodness when all my experience was of rejection, faith in life when I only expected death, faith in God, who had been given back to me, not as a monster, but as an inexhaustible source of love for me, an outcast. If I never met him again, I would follow this man for the rest of my life. He restored to me all that was precious – love, life, God – and myself, body and spirit. He wiped the marks of my sin from my flesh.

I know now that in one way I will always be alone. I have been through experiences that few have shared, and that set me apart from my fellows. I have been to the edge of death and looked over. But now I do not mind the loneliness so much. I would rather be alone than belong within a group which only has its existence by keeping others out. And other people have almost as much difficulty accepting me as one who has been healed, as they did me as one who was sick. There is even a little of what seems like awe in their faces. What a world we live in, that hates the broken, yet fears the whole. It is not my changed body that seems to mystify them so much as the spirit they can sense is unbound in a way it never was before, even before I was ill.

I think I saw something of the same aloneness in *his* eyes, when he asked me why the others had not come back. The men of his own race and religion have been slow to recognize him, even the ones he has helped. That must cause him great hurt. And I feel for this man I love, for all the rejection and fear he must suffer. But then I remember how he laughed with me, and put his arm round me, and I hope that, wherever he is, he knows that the love and the courage he has given to poor, broken people like me, to resist everything that would make us less than human, has given us life. And that the knowledge helps him to keep going. I think it will. I think he is very close to God.

So I live, alone. But I know now that there are others like me, who have had the iron band cut from them, whose spirits have been set free. Sometimes, I meet them, and we recognize one another. Soon, I must go and do what I can with my knowledge. Things are a little better for us now. Some people are finding the courage to speak out on our behalf, to face their ignorance and dispel some of the myths. But there is still a long, long way to go. I don't know how long I will live, or in what manner I will die. But for now, God has given my life back to me, and I must use it. And very soon, I will. In the meantime, it is still enough to wake up in the morning, and to breathe, and see the red balloon soar up into the sky, and be carried far, far away on the breeze. It is enough to breathe, and to give thanks to God.

* * *

The leprosy stories in the Gospels are interesting; people believed that leprosy was a punishment from God for sin. So as well as the terrible fear of and ignorance about the disease, lepers were doubly outcast, as those who had committed some awful sin. They were forbidden to come near people, received little or no care, and lived on what they could gather and the charity of a few kind souls. Their existence must have been one of the utmost misery. I cannot read this story without thinking of those who are the new lepers in our society, those whose lives are plagued by the same fear and ignorance. We are more enlightened nowadays about the leprosy that is still a scourge in some countries, but those with AIDS face a life as outcasts.

I also find this story interesting because it goes on to describe the response of those who were healed, and how only one of them, a foreigner, a member of the hated and despised Samaritan race, came back to show his gratitude to Jesus, a fact which was important enough for Jesus to mention it, with perhaps a note of sadness in his question about his own people.

Some questions to help your own imagining of this story:

1 How do you imagine it would have felt to be a leper?

2 Have you ever been treated this way?
3 Where do *you* see people being treated like lepers were treated?
4 What strikes you about Jesus' response to these men?
5 What is *your* response when you meet someone who is in a similar situation?

The belief that illness or disability was a punishment for sin was a strong one in Jesus' society. Read the story of Jesus healing a man born blind, found in John 9, in which Jesus makes it clear that the man's blindness had nothing to do with either his or his parents' sin. Though it is a long passage, it is worth imagining how it might happen now, because it goes into detail about the effect this healing had, not only on the man, but on the whole community. Imagine how you, and the people in *your* community would react if this happened to a blind person living among you.

4. The Lost Son

'Everything I have is yours'
LUKE 15.11–32

Jesus went on to say: 'There was once a man who had two sons. The younger one said to him, "Father, give me my share of the property now." So the man divided his property between his two sons. After a few days the younger son sold his part of the property and left home with the money. He went to a country far away, where he wasted his money in reckless living. He spent everything he had. Then a severe famine spread over that country, and he was left without a thing. So he went to work for one of the citizens of that country, who sent him out to his farm to take care of the pigs. He wished he could fill himself with the bean pods the pigs ate, but no one gave him anything to eat. At last he came to his senses and said, "All my father's hired workers have more than they can eat, and here I am about to starve! I will get up and go to my father and say, Father, I have sinned against God and against you. I am no longer fit to be called your son; treat me as one of your hired workers." So he got up and started back to his father.

'He was still a long way from home when his father saw him; his heart was filled with pity, and he ran, threw his arms round his son, and kissed him. "Father," the son said, "I have sinned against God and against you. I am no longer fit to be called your son." But the father called his servants. "Hurry", he said. "Bring the best robe and put it on him. Put a ring on his finger and shoes on his feet. Then go and get the prize calf and kill it, and let us celebrate with a feast! For this son of mine was dead, but now he is alive; he was lost, but now he has been found." And so the feasting began.

'In the meantime the elder son was out in the field. On his way back, when he came close to the house, he heard the music and dancing. So he called one of the servants and asked him, "What's going on?" "Your brother has come back home," the servant answered, "and your father has killed the prize calf, because he got him back safe and sound."

'The elder brother was so angry that he would not go into the house; so his father came out and begged him to come in. But he answered his father, "Look, all these years I have worked for you like a slave, and I have never disobeyed your orders. What have you given me? Not even a goat for me to have a feast with my friends! But this son of yours wasted all your property on prostitutes, and when he comes back home, you kill the prize calf for him!" "My son," the father answered, "you are always here with me, and everything I have is yours. But we had to celebrate and be happy, because your brother was dead, but now he is alive; he was lost, but now he has been found."'

Once upon a time, there was a man who was very unhappy. The reasons for his unhappiness were complex, and he didn't understand them very well himself. He worked in a family business with his father, and the business was very prosperous, so he had few financial problems. He worked extremely hard, didn't take much time off and, all in all, took life rather seriously. However, to the casual observer, he was a successful man, honest, upright and decent. He had a younger brother, the black sheep of the family. Several years before, this brother had wheedled a large sum of money out of his father and disappeared abroad. He never wrote home, but they heard from gossip that he was living a fairly dissipated life, throwing drunken parties, experimenting with drugs, and with a different woman every week. The older brother knew how much his father had been hurt when the boy ran out on them, and knew also how much his mother worried about the son from whom she never heard. And their pain, because he loved them, showed itself in him as a kind of contemptuous toleration. But, secretly mixed in with that, was a little sneaking envy for his brother who was having a good time in the sun while he clocked up his eight hours and more each day in the business.

When the family heard, again as a result of gossiping neighbours, that the younger son had gone through all his money and had made a swift descent to the bottom, the man felt a grim satisfaction. The thought of him living in some squalid slum after the luxury apartments, queuing up for the leftovers at the back door of hotel kitchens, abandoned by his fair-weather friends, had a certain poetic justice about it. But, once in a while, a memory came unsought to his mind of a little bright-eyed boy who was always getting into mischief and running to his big brother to protect him, and at these times a kind of heavy sadness settled on his heart, which never really went completely away.

One day the man had to go away for a business meeting connected with a new product the company was marketing. The trip was long and tiring, and he didn't get back till the middle of the evening, feeling hot, uncomfortable and wanting nothing more than to have a relaxing bath and to get into bed. As he approached the house he saw that every room was brightly lit up, and music was carrying on the night air over the garden and into the street. There were many people coming and going from the house, carrying bottles and laughing and talking excitedly. It was clear that a party was taking place. This was such an unusual occurrence in a house which was usually so quiet and sedate, a house, moreover, which he had left that morning with no mention of such an event, that he stopped for a moment in amazement. As his tired mind searched for an explanation, one of his father's employees came out of the house, obviously in cheerful mood. The elder brother quickened his step, and caught the man by his arm. 'What on earth's happening here?' he asked. The man turned, startled, and then relaxed, seeing who it was. 'Oh, it's you', he said. 'You gave me quite a shock there.' 'Nothing like the shock I'm having', muttered the elder brother. 'What's going on? When I left this morning, no one said anything to me about a party. Anyway, there hasn't been a party in this house for I don't know how long – the last time there were a lot of people here was when Uncle Willie died six years ago.'

The other man, slightly befuddled, but full of the spirit of fellowship, said, with the air of one bearing good news, 'It's your brother, Jack, you know. Well of course you know, don't you, he's *your* brother. He's come home. Turned up this morning after hitching all the way from the coast. Quite a sight he was too – filthy dirty, smelling to high heaven, wearing tennis shoes with holes in them, in this weather too. And really looking as if he's been through the mill – looks as if he's been ill, I'd say. I think your mother got a real fright when she saw him. I was at the office with your father at the Friday planning meeting when she phoned to say he'd come home. Well, I've never seen your old man move like that. He was off like a shot, into the car and home, just stopping on the way to pick up some new clothes for your brother from the High Street. He was like a man who's just been let out of prison. Then, later on in the afternoon, he phoned in and told Jenny that he was having a party tonight, and everyone was welcome, especially anyone who knew Jack. Well, of course, half the folk in this firm were at school with him. They all knew that he was living the high life, and I think they were curious to see what kind of state he was in, with it all having gone sour on him. And besides there were a lot who just wanted to see him. He was always a sociable kind of chap, always ready for a laugh.

'So we all rolled up tonight, and your folks certainly have pulled out all the stops. There's enough food in there to feed an army, and your father's going round with a bottle of his best malt whisky, pouring out nips for anyone who'll take them. And Jack's sitting there in the middle of it all looking as if he doesn't know *what's* going on, as if he thinks that if he blinks too hard, it'll all disappear. I don't know, maybe he was a bit scared to come back, maybe he thought your old

The Lost Son

man would come the stern father act and show him the door. But anyone can see they're just thrilled to have him back. Anyway, I have to get home, I'm playing golf first thing tomorrow morning, can't be out too late. Away in and join the party – they'll be going for hours yet, you're not too late.' And with a cheery wave, he walked off down the road.

The elder brother stood quite still. He could feel his legs start to shake, and a hot wave of anger sweep over him. He stood while the rage of years possessed him with a violence that terrified him with its power. All the pent-up resentment of the brother who had broken free of the bonds of duty, all the anxiety of his mother and the disappointment of his father, all the gnawing envy of his brother who let people down all the time, and yet was the popular, the sought-after one, welled up inside him so that he could not move. The front door opened, and a figure came out. It was his father, who had seen the elder son's car draw up. He looked around, then caught sight of the dark figure standing motionless by the gate. He came towards him and, seeing his twisted face, knew that his son had discovered what had happened. He said nothing for a moment, then said quietly, 'Jack's come home. Come on in and see him.'

The elder brother looked at his father blindly, scarcely seeming to see him. 'Why should I come in?', he said harshly. 'Why should I come to his party? For years I've been the obedient son, the good little boy, the reliable worker. For years I've done what's been expected of me; I've never been in trouble, I've never embarrassed you with the neighbours; and what thanks have I got? You never threw a party for me, or made a fuss of me like this. You never even suggested that I should invite my friends round for a special occasion. I'm just like some part of the furniture. And now Jack's come crawling home looking like something from under a stone, having run through all your money, made a laughing-stock of himself and mixed with God knows what kind of riff-raff. And you welcome him with open arms as if he'd never been away.' His voice cracked with resentment and humiliation, and he could say nothing else.

His father looked at him compassionately, for he was a just man, and he recognized the truth in what his son said. By all normal standards, it wasn't fair. And he knew his son was hurt. He thought of all the times he and his wife had worried about this elder son of theirs, so private, so intense, so serious. He had never brought friends home to the house, or come home noisy and cheerful with the milkman, and they had assumed it was because he had wished it otherwise. They had thought that he was satisfied by spending his spare time reading quietly at home, or listening to music in his room, or occasionally going to a concert with a colleague. Now it seemed that they might have been wrong after all, so hurt did he seem to be, particularly over the question of a party. He thought of his younger son, wild, irresponsible, living on his charm and popularity, and now reduced to the gutter, and he looked at the hurt man standing before him, and he sighed the sigh of all parents, who bring children into the world and then agonize over how best to show their love for them, a task that only got more complex as they got older. So many times he and his wife had wondered where they had gone wrong with their children, the one so wilful and selfish, the other so serious, but so hard to get close to.

Then he thought about Jack as he had seen him today, almost unrecognizable, not just because of the beard and the filth and the thinness, but changed on other ways. There was something in his eyes that had not been there before – as if he had seen things that had frightened him, as if he had had a glimpse of hell. His voice seemed gentler, more hesitant, and his whole manner was unsure, lacking in confidence – Jack, who before could charm the birds off the trees. He had greeted his father like a remorseful child, and his father's heart had gone out to him with a love that transcended all notions of equity. Yes, Jack had been changed for ever by what had happened to him. Well their task was clear for them now. The cockiness was gone, but he thought that it wasn't too late for the brightness to come back to his eyes. He had hope for Jack now.

But this other son, this locked-in child of thirty. Was there hope there too? He said gently, 'Son, this is your home. You're a part of everything we are and everything we do. You're not part of the furniture, but you are part of the foundation. You're my colleague, and I depend on you. And everything – the business, the house, everything I have is yours too, to choose what you do with it. But your mother and I, we had to be happy and celebrate, we couldn't do anything else, because your brother came back to us. We thought he was lost to us for ever, but we've found him again. And he's changed. He's been through Hell, and it's left its mark on him, but now he's back in our lives again. We have to be happy.'

Then he put his hand on his son's shoulder, turned away, and walked back into the house.

The elder son went and sat down on the garden seat. The emotions which he had controlled so rigidly for years had finally mastered him, and the rage which he had spent on his father had been replaced by an even more difficult feeling for him to cope with. He could feel the tears burning the back of his eyes, and his throat hurt from trying to suppress them. He took a deep breath of night air and let go, and the tears began to run unheeded down his cheeks.

He sat for a long time, while the noise of the party went on, while his anger receded and he tried to make sense of the pain inside him. His father's words came back to him over and over again, 'everything I have is yours', and the loving and concerned tone in which they had been spoken. Gradually, his own sense of justice reasserted itself. The party thing had hurt most, and he knew that he had often wished to be part of the brightness and the warmth and the spontaneity. But he acknowledged to himself that he had been afraid of parties – afraid to expose himself in front of strangers, afraid of being made to look a fool, afraid of taking the risk of trying something new and different – risks which Jack had been prepared to take. And who was to say that Jack hadn't been just as fearful, with the same dry throat, the fear of rejection, the same moment of panic before entering a crowded room. But Jack had taken the risks – and now, it seemed, alas, paid some of the price. He, on the other hand, had covered up his fear, pretended he didn't care about parties, that he despised them, so that eventually, even if he'd wanted, no one would have believed him if he'd invited them to one.

Then he thought about being taken for granted, being part of the furniture. Perhaps he was, but, if so, it was a mutual understanding. He thought of everything that surrounded him, which he, too, took for granted – the meals that came on time, the comfort of his home, the security of belonging to a group of people with common goals, work which was often grinding and dull, but gave him a sense of accomplishment, the quiet of his own room at night – all the blessed ordinariness of daily life, all resting on the strength of his parents' love. He thought about his brother, and why he had thought it necessary to escape from all that. He had never gone any further than imagining it to be his brother's selfishness. But perhaps there was something about a restless boy who had fallen into scrapes from infancy feeling in some way unworthy of all the love that surrounded him, about a younger brother who felt inadequate beside the older brother who always did everything right, and always had to rescue him from trouble. Perhaps he simply could not cope with the expectations of those who loved him, and had gone off to prove his unworthiness. He thought suddenly that now Jack wouldn't need to do that any more. His parents' welcome had proved that they didn't love him because he was worthy, they just loved him.

And himself. His father had said, 'Everything I have is yours'. And that then included his love. Not because he worked hard, or was a good son, but just because it was there. In spite of himself, he smiled ruefully. Jack with his unworthiness, he with his worthiness, both needing to be loved. And it didn't make a blind bit of difference with either of them. Their parents loved them for the men they were, not for what they should be. Perhaps knowing that, he could stop trying so hard to be perfect, perhaps Jack could stay in a place where he didn't feel judged all the time. Perhaps Jack could teach him to be a little more uninhibited, if he hadn't lost the taste for frivolity altogether (which he hoped he hadn't). What could he teach Jack? He wasn't so sure that someone as blind as he was the best person to teach anybody anything. But maybe there would be something.

He thought about his father, and how, tonight, in spite of everything, he suddenly looked ten years younger. He imagined his mother's shining face. And he thought about his brother – the child always in trouble, the rebellious young man – and now what? He got up from the seat and, from long habit, straightened his tie. Then he smiled, took it off, and went in the door.

*   *   *

One of the great offences of the Gospel is that it seems unfair. Fairness demands an appropriate reward for good actions. Jesus, on the other hand, rewarded with his presence and friendship wastrels, scoundrels and profligates, while remaining seemingly oblivious to the claims of the respectable and respected. It is a paradox of the church today that it seems often to be composed largely of the respectable and respected, fearful of the claims of the wretched (or, at least, the undeserving wretched). And the people Jesus claimed as his own were most certainly undeserving. The message, the secret of God, is clearly reserved to the undeserving. It is the message, the secret, of mercy, which is the ultimate quality of God in Christ. 'The great love she has shown proves that her many sins have been forgiven. But whoever has been forgiven little shows only a little love.'

But what of the respectable and respected? How does the secret become real to us also, how is the quality of mercy born in us also when we are still worried over the demands of fairness? Perhaps the answer lies in our ability to appreciate all that we already have, and in our thankfulness to find generosity of spirit.

Some questions to help your own imagining of this story:

1 Who in the story do you identify with most?
2 What is it that causes you to do so?
3 Where do you see generosity of spirit being shown around you?
4 What do you take for granted in your life?

Another story which raises questions of equity and generosity is the parable of the workers in the vineyard, in Matthew 20.1-16. Jesus had a deep commitment to economic justice, so the story cannot simply be understood as a kind of 'union-bashing' parable. Try to imagine the story from the point of view of one of the workers hired early in the day, and think of it as taking place in your town.

5. The Pharisee and the Tax Collector

'Not . . . like everybody else.'
LUKE 18.9–14

Jesus also told this parable to people who were sure of their own goodness and despised everybody else. 'Once there were two men who went up to the Temple to pray: one was a Pharisee, the other a tax collector.

'The Pharisee stood apart by himself and prayed, "I thank you, God, that I am not greedy, dishonest, or an adulterer like everyone else. I thank you that I am not like that tax collector over there. I fast two days a week, and I give you a tenth of all my income."

'But the tax collector stood at a distance and would not even raise his face to heaven, but beat on his breast and said, "God, have pity on me, a sinner!" I tell you' said Jesus, 'the tax collector, and not the Pharisee, was in the right with God when he went home.

The Pharisee and the Tax Collector 47

For everyone who makes himself great will be humbled, and everyone who humbles himself will be made great.'

Two men went into a church to pray. They were called Mr Smith and Mr Jones.

Mr Smith knew his way around, so he immediately walked straight forward to the front of the church, slipped into a pew in the first row, and, with the contented sigh of someone who knows himself to be in the right place, sat down. After a few moments spent drinking in the quiet and tranquil atmosphere of the old stones, the polished wood and the gleaming candlesticks, he knelt to pray.

Mr Jones, on the other hand, had not been in a church for a very long time, consequently he was, and looked, extremely uncomfortable. He peered nervously round him, as if he expected some figure of authority to appear any minute and tell him he had no business to be there. He seemed unsure of where to sit, and if there was any special ritual he should observe before committing himself to stay. Finally, he slid cautiously into the very back row, in the corner furthest away from the altar. In that shadowy corner, he crumpled up, his legs tucked away under the pew, his head hanging down over his knees, and tried to hide.

Meanwhile, up at the front, Mr Smith was reviewing his life, as he did every week. Mr Smith was a man who took his faith very seriously, and he tried most conscientiously to do what was right. You could tell that just by looking at him. He didn't believe in killing animals for human gratification, so, as well as being a strict vegetarian (who had been known to refuse an entire dinner because he wasn't satisfied about the nature of the margarine it had been cooked in), he never wore leather shoes, and walked the streets in interesting canvas sandals, except when it was wet, when he wore a pair of rather ancient wellingtons. His sweater was obviously hand-knitted (he believed in encouraging local craft skills) and his trousers looked as if they had been bought in an Oxfam shop (which indeed they had). Mr Smith thought it was a sign of an underdeveloped conscience (or even mind) to be concerned with such trivial things as appearance. The whole fashion industry, he believed, was merely a means for capitalists to exploit the wish for colour and fantasy of the poor, and a way of diverting their energies from the struggle for economic justice and political engagement. As an antidote to this, Mr Smith was presently engaged in a scheme to bring Central American and African skills of art and banner-making to the housing scheme where he was a development officer. Or rather, as he called it, 'worker' (the term 'officer' had much too military a ring to it).

Mr Jones's clothes, unfortunately, were exactly a case in point for Mr Smith. He was wearing a leather jacket. He was wearing very fashionable corduroy trousers. He was wearing an Italian designer sweater. He was wearing a gold watch, a gold ring, and a thin gold chain round his neck. He had an expensive haircut, of the kind that needs to be trimmed every two weeks to keep it in shape. Mr Smith had summed him up in two minutes as they entered the church together, with his acutely refined political sensibility, as a person whose consciousness was not raised.

Mr Jones had not noticed Mr Smith's screening as he entered the church. In fact, he had barely noticed Mr Smith at all. He was much too miserable.

As may be gathered, Mr Smith took pride in his ability to avoid falling prey to the lures of consumerism. His university education had given him a deep contempt for the weakness of those people who seemed unable to do without 'things', and whose sense of the deeper joys of life was therefore dulled. But he knew that they were simply victims of iniquitous systems and structures, and therefore he laboured long and hard to lift the burden of oppression off the backs of his fellow men and women. As he reflected on the week that had gone, he permitted himself a modest glow of pleasure at the success of his plan to restructure the entire development scheme for his area. Of course, it would involve all of them in a lot of extra work, and possibly even in giving up a couple of evenings a week, but this was a sacrifice he was perfectly prepared to make. Following on his successful campaign to have smoking banned completely in the community centre, and his uncovering of the culprit involved in the petty thefts from the office (a janitor who immediately got the sack – one thing if it had been kids from

The Pharisee and the Tax Collector

deprived homes, but this was a man who could afford to take holidays abroad), he felt he had some justification for feeling pretty pleased with the way things were going.

Mr Jones, still sunk in despair in the corner, had no justification at all for feeling pleased with how things were going at work. He had just discovered that the old woman whose furniture they had repossessed after she fell behind with her repayments, had put her head in the gas oven. (It was the shame, her neighbours said.)

Mr Smith's thoughts turned with affection to his wife. Or, as he often thought about her, his partner in collegiality. They had got things worked out pretty well, he thought contentedly. His flexible hours, which allowed him to take mornings off in lieu of the evenings he worked, meant that he could look after the children in the mornings while she did her course on the psychology of religious rites in tribal societies. Then he could hand over to her, and of course, they shared the housework equally. He often felt he was striking a blow for the liberation of the human species from role stereotyping when he took his children to the mother and toddlers group in the church hall, and he knew it would not be long before the young women who went there got over their rather juvenile habit of giggling and then lapsing into silence whenever he arrived. He and his wife didn't see each other as much as they might have, but they knew it was important that each of them be fulfilled as independent persons, and that she not be seen just as 'his wife'. They got along pretty well, all in all, and he had certainly never been tempted to indulge in any extra-marital fun, as some of his colleagues did. It just wouldn't be worth the bother.

Mr Jones's love life wasn't going too well either. The woman he was living with had just thrown him out, when her patience with him had finally worn thin. You couldn't blame her, really. He knew that he drank too much, and that when he was drunk, he said and did things he always regretted later. And he knew that she didn't like his friends, who were casual with women, and the law. And he knew, most of all, that he shouldn't have hit her last night. He hadn't hit her hard, but he had seen the look of disgust and fear and sadness on her face when he lifted his hand, and a great wave of misery and self-loathing had carried his arm down across her head. Of course, he had been drinking, and the final straw had been seeing her in the pub with that other man, the stranger. She had said he was just a friend, and she wasn't one to tell lies, but he could see the shape of things to come. She deserved some one better than him. And in all of it, he could not find the words to tell her how much he loved her. He was not comfortable talking about love. But he yearned for her, for a way to make it all right again, and he yearned for the kid. He would miss the kid terribly. The vast loneliness and helplessness of it all convulsed him, and he wept into his hands.

Mr Smith gazed round the church, and his mind turned to the meeting he would be attending here tonight. He felt strongly the importance of the church's role in the struggle. People had spiritual dimensions to their lives which could only be ignored at the risk of a serious psychological imbalance, and here he knew he had to disagree with his Marxist colleagues. Though he regretted the tendency in many believers to wish to retain elements in their faith which were, quite frankly, superstitious, and found distasteful the way in which they wanted to use the church as a kind of comforter, a warm blanket to protect them from reality, nevertheless he saw the church's potential to be a kind of radical spiritual fighting force, thundering against the injustices of society and confronting the corruption of government, which was far too accommodating of the materialism from that empire to the West. So he fought a persistent battle, a crusade, you might almost call it, in the church, trying to drag it into the twentieth century, attempting to wean his fellow-members away from their petty concerns and obsessions with the Sunday School, the Women's Guild, the need for more hospital visiting and the state of the roof. Oh yes, he felt strongly about the importance of his role in the church. He was, without being arrogant about it, the church's conscience, raising up the issues they would rather forget.

Mr Jones had not been in a church for many years. The last time he could remember had been for a family wedding, when he had felt uncomfortable and out of place. He still didn't understand what had made him come in now. In his wretchedness, it had been as much an instinct as anything, like a wounded rabbit bolting for cover. Somewhere to hide, a sanctuary, a place of safety in the storm. He knew he had no right to be in here, where the good people came. There was nothing good about him. His life was a mess. He hurt the people he loved. Other people hated his job, and he hated it too. But he liked the money it gave him, and, if he was honest, he liked the little bit of power it gave him too. No, nothing good about him at all. It would be no loss to anyone if, one day, he just disappeared, lost from the human race. The thought of his lostness, his nothingness terrified him, and his mind slid into a black pit, out of which a small voice seemed to cry, 'Help me, God. I'm sorry, God. Help me, God.'

Mr Smith, having finished his weekly rendering, noticed Mr Jones again, and marked that he seemed to be in some distress. He was not too inclined to feel sympathy for him. Someone who could afford to dress the way he did had to be involved somehow in exploiting the poor. He had chosen his own path, and if he was learning the hard way that it didn't bring him satisfaction, then perhaps it would be a salutary lesson. Mr Jones sniffled out loud, and a slight frisson of revulsion ran through Mr Smith. He thanked God that he would never find himself slumped in a corner in a church, snivelling and without dignity. His duty was clear, and he could follow it through, without compromise and without fear. To struggle on behalf of the poor and oppressed was an honourable way of life, and one which afforded him much spiritual reward. A tiny flicker of unease crept into his thoughts, a tiny question about why he often found himself a little uncomfortable in the presence of the poor people he worked amongst; not so much in his job, but when he, as he sometimes did, went into the local pub to share their leisure. Sitting with his half-pint, he sometimes had the faintest suspicion that they didn't like him, even that they were laughing at him. Well, if that was the case, so be it. You couldn't always expect people to appreciate what you were doing on their behalf, or, indeed, always to understand what was best for them. If this was the price he had to pay, then he would pay it. He was confident that he was doing what God wanted, and that eventually, justice would triumph and the oppressors would be cast down. So he prayed.

As Mr Smith and Mr Jones prayed, each in his own way, God (naturally) was giving a keen ear to their prayers. And being one who was easily (some said naively) moved to pity, God's heart went out to Mr Jones, who was obviously wretched, and in need of all the love and support and guidance he could get. What God really wanted to do for Mr Jones was to catch him up in a warm, motherly embrace, and hold him there for a while until he had let go of all his fears and shame, and had the confidence to venture out timidly once more into the big world. Just like an old hen with her chicks, really. But of course, that wasn't possible (and, not for the first time, God wondered about the wisdom of leaving human beings alone to get on with one another and make decisions for themselves – it sometimes made one feel remarkably frustrated), so God started to think about the list of those who might be pulled in, and encouraged to help poor Mr Jones with his problems. There was bound to be someone. There always was, when you put your mind to it, and this was the one thing that could be relied on to relieve God's sense of helplessness.

But even God's well-known tolerance and long-suffering was rather stretched by Mr Smith, and one had to admit to just the tiniest bit of irritation with him.

'Can't for the life of me imagine what he's doing in here, talking to me', muttered God. 'Doesn't need me in the slightest. Got everything all sewn up, hasn't he? Doesn't really need anyone, come to that. Well, he seems to know what he's doing, I don't expect he'd appreciate me interfering with his plan for the human race. He'd probably think I was soft in the head if I told him how much I love Mr Jones, undeserving irreligious wretch that he is.'

Then God's sense of natural justice reasserted itself. 'One has to admit, he's not putting a foot wrong. One has to give him credit for trying.' Then, naughtily, 'and he certainly is very trying. Oh dear, I must stop this. I hope all his plans work out for him. There's bound to be a nice human being there somewhere underneath all that self-righteousness. After all, I did make him, and it's there in everybody somewhere. Perhaps one of these days, there'll

The Pharisee and the Tax Collector

be something I can do for him. I *do* like to be able to help. But he certainly doesn't need me just now. Oh well. . .now, where had I got to with dear Mr Jones. . .?'

*   *   *

There are many stories in the Gospels in which Jesus contrasts the response to God of the pious and respectable with that of the disreputable and despised. It must have been scandalous to the first group (those we call in Scotland the 'unco guid'), to hear Jesus say that the tax-collectors and prostitutes would enter the Kingdom of God in front of them. And yet in the church today so many of us are respectable, so few of us numbered among the tax-collectors and prostitutes. Perhaps, as in the story, the difference is in our need of God. The Pharisee was self-sufficient, did his duty, kept all of the religious laws. And yet there was something missing in his prayers – the humility that stems from knowing the extent of human weakness in us. There is something of the Pharisee in almost all of us, though it may be expressed in many different kinds of self-righteous attitudes. So a big question this story raises for me is: when the does the desire to do what is right and good spill over into the desire to justify myself by comparison with others – and why?

Some questions to help your own imagining of this story:

1 What is *your* picture of a Pharisee or a tax-collector?
2 The Pharisee was proud because he did the right things, while the tax-collector was ashamed because he did the wrong things. What are the things that people tend to be proud of today?
3 Is it ever right to be proud of what you have done?
4 What reinforces the Pharisee in you?

The Pharisee's good opinion of himself rewarded him for doing what was right. The passage in Luke 14.7-14 is a description of righteousness which does not seek rewards. Imagine who *you* would invite to a dinner like the one Jesus describes, by name, if you can.

6. The Killing of the Children

'For they are all dead'
MATTHEW 2.16-18

When Herod realized that the visitors from the East had tricked him, he was furious. He gave orders to kill all the boys in Bethlehem and its neighbourhood who were two years old and younger - this was done in accordance with what he had learned from the visitors about the time when the star had appeared.

In this way, what the prophet Jeremiah had said came true: 'A sound is heard in Ramah, the sound of bitter weeping. Rachel is crying for her children; she refuses to be comforted, for they are dead.'

NO! GOD! NO!
 I can't breathe. I can't breathe. Get away from me. I can't

The Killing of the Children

breathe. Don't stop me, get your hands off me, don't touch me. DON'T TOUCH MY BABY! . . . BASTARDS!

They killed my baby. He's dead! Look at all the blood. He's dead. DON'T TOUCH ME! You'll get blood all over your clothes. He's got a big hole in his chest. Look at the blood. He's dead. Why is he dead? Why did they kill him? He's just a baby!

They're all just babies. They killed all the babies. All the baby boys. Where's my mother? I want my mother. Someone get my mother. Please. Mama, please come quickly, I need you.

Oh Mama, they killed my baby. He's getting cold, and I can't warm him up . . . The soldiers did it. They came just a little while ago. There were a lot of them. They killed all the baby boys, in every house in the village. Where were you? I was in the house, getting the dinner ready. I remember, I was cutting up vegetables. The children were playing just outside the house. The baby was sitting on the ground, playing with some stones, piling them up and pushing them over. His sister was there too, keeping an eye on him. She was sitting just near him, singing one of her funny songs. And he kept falling over, and every time he fell over, she sat him back up again. The village was quite quiet. Just a few children playing around outside, waiting for their fathers to come back from the fields. It was so peaceful – you know how it is here, sometimes, just when the sun's going down. Oh Mama, look at my baby, he's so small. Two hours ago I was nursing him, and he was alive and warm, oh Mama. Then the soldiers came, oh yes, it was the militia, it wasn't any of our men. You know what they're like. They came quickly, they must have had transport hidden just outside the village, because they came so quietly, one moment there was nobody, and the next, they were there, all over the place.

I was still in the house when I heard Maria scream, and scream and scream. I knew something was wrong – if she had fallen and hurt herself, you know how she always whines, but it wasn't like that. She just screamed and screamed like an animal in a trap. I rushed outside, it must just have been seconds, and there was a man grabbing the baby off the front step, with Maria hanging on to his clothes, and he was swinging her off her feet but she wouldn't let go. Just as I came out, he swung his arm round behind him and gave her a terrible thump, and she fell off crying. He had the baby in his arms, trying to shift him on to one arm so he could bring up this awful knife-thing, like a machete, that he had in his other hand. I threw myself at him spitting like a cat, and tearing at him, to get my baby back. And just out of the corner of my eye I could see the soldiers rushing into a whole lot of other houses, and women screaming, and people spilling out of the houses, but it was like all that was going on in a dream somewhere. It wasn't real, and I was hanging on to the soldier and screaming and shouting at him, and hitting him and scratching him, and trying to get his eyes. And he was cursing and swearing, and trying to get his knife free with one hand, and hold on to the baby and hit me with the other hand. It was hard to see his face, he was moving around and it was all happening so fast, and I could hear myself yelling at him. I didn't know I could shout so loud. Then he dropped the baby. Quite deliberately. He just let him go, and he bounced down in the dust, and lay there crying with his face all crumpled up. I let go the man to bend down and pick him up. Before I got to him, oh God, it all happened so quickly, he hit me with the side of his arm, a great heavy blow, and it took me off my feet, and I fell and hit my head on the ground. And when I tried to get up, he kicked me in the stomach. And then I just had to watch it, oh God, Mama, it all happened so quickly, I was up on my knees trying to stand up and Maria was running to me crying and crying and he bent down and stuck his knife into the baby like he was opening a sack of potatoes, and then he did it again, and I was kneeling there begging him not to do it and he did it again and it was like the knife was going into me. Why wasn't it me? Why wasn't it me?

He stood there for a minute, looking at the baby. I suppose, to make sure he was dead. And I looked at him. He had a peculiar expression on his face. It looked . . . squeezed. And I said to him, or I think I whispered, 'Why?' And he shouted at me.

'We know all about you people. Sheltering terrorists and revolutionaries. We know about you.' And I said, and I think

The Killing of the Children

at that point I was quite calm and not scared any more, 'But he was just a baby. He was only eight months old.' And the soldier said, 'But he would've grown up to be one of them. He might have turned out to be a leader, a subversive, a communist.'

Then I spat at him. I felt such hatred. I thought he was the lowest form of life, to say such things. He turned to go away, and I screamed after him, 'Haven't you got any children?', and he kind of stopped, and shouted without turning round, 'I'm just obeying orders.'

It was the same all through the village. Every house that had a baby boy in it, even the ones who were toddling around, they chased them into the houses and dragged them from their mothers' arms. They took a baby who was three days old, three days old, Mama, and slit its throat. Oh Mama, it's the end of life, Mama, I want to die. They killed a couple of girl babies as well because they couldn't be bothered to check the sex. The woman two houses along's gone into labour and she's only six months gone. That'll be another baby to die. I think they went to some other villages as well.

This place is like hell. When the men came back, there were all these dead babies, and women screaming everywhere, and children crying and dogs barking and the grandmothers wandering around rubbing dirt into their faces and hair, and one or two with basins and cloths trying to clear up the mess. That would make you laugh, wouldn't it? This village will never be clean again. They'll never stop the blood. Damn God. There's no God. If there was a god, he wouldn't let this happen. Or maybe we're being punished. Punished for being poor, and defenceless, and for wanting things to be better for our children. Except I haven't got children now. This morning I had children. I curse God, I will hate him for ever. I don't care if he does hear me, where was he when all this was happening, and what does his precious holy law say about this? I haven't got a husband any more, I haven't got a son any more, I haven't got anything any more.

They must have been after someone. Usually it's the silent visit in the night, the knock at the door, the dark shadow bundled out of the house, and then nothing. No word, silence, for weeks, until a body shows up dumped somewhere with its face cut off. They must have been after someone. I hope they got him. I hope he's somewhere being tortured to death, because he wasn't worth all these babies' lives. I hope his mother suffers like I am. I hope she's alive to see her baby that she carried for nine months, and sweated and groaned to bring into this hellish life, and washed and dressed and rocked and sang to and nursed and went short for and played with and prayed for, and gave a name to and LOVED – I hope she lives to see his body battered and bloody and hold him cold in her arms.

No I don't. I hope he got away. I hope he's a thousand miles away, and that they're sweating with fear because they didn't get him. I hope he comes back to haunt them, and threaten them, and that they never get a night's sleep again because of him. I hope that monster in his fancy palace with his fancy guards and his fancy women and his foreign money spends the rest of his life watching his back. I hope that whoever it was they were looking for lives for ever, so that they don't ever forget this night, and nobody ever forgets it . . .

Oh Mama, I'm so tired now, I think I'll just go to sleep. I'll just lie down here with my baby, he needs his mother, we'll just go to sleep together, and then we'll wake up in the morning with the sun coming through the trees and it'll all have been a dream. Oh Mama, please let us lie down here, it doesn't matter if it's outside, we don't mind the cold, my baby and me. We want to sleep and forget and not wake up, Mama. Please let me lie down, oh Mama, no, please don't take my baby away, let me keep him, oh Mama, no, please, no, Mama . . .

Is that you, Mama? Where's my baby, where have they taken him? They've taken him away and I don't know where they've laid him, Mama. Who's that? You're not Mama . . . Maria, Maria. My daughter. Maria.

Oh darling, don't cry, come and see Mama, come and have a big cuddle, you come and lie down beside me, and we'll have a kiss. You were such a good girl today, you were so brave. Come on, Maria, come to Mama. We have to look after each other now, don't we? Come to Mama . . .

* * *

The Killing of the Children

As the mother of young children, I find it all too easy to imagine the agony of such a senseless slaughter. The shock, the fear, the anger and the hopeless desolation come vividly, and yet I know that the reality must far surpass the worst of my imaginings. The families who were so bereaved must have hardly understood why this was happening to them at all, perhaps attributed it to the unpredictable whim of a cruel and capricious ruler. In these circumstances, it would be understandable for women to cry 'My God, why have you forsaken me?', to curse God and despair. I find it hard to deal with the paradox which places the tender and glorious accounts of the birth of Jesus in the same context as this tragedy. I want to ask God, 'Why did this have to happen?' And yet I know that it demonstrates that the incarnation did not take place in some fairy-tale world of long ago, where everything was happy and innocent, but in the real, brutal world where even the innocent, and sometimes especially the innocent, are done to death. It was to that world that Jesus came, and suffered the same fate – except that for him, it was a freely-chosen obedience that led him out to die.

Perhaps the saddest thing about this story for me is the fact that it is so easy to imagine it happening today. It does, has, happened time and time again, just this century. It is the experience of women in Germany, in Russia, in Vietnam, in Southern Africa, in Central America. It is the Mothers of the Disappeared in Argentina. And so, for me, Rachel weeping for her children is all of these women – real, individual, suffering women, and yet also a symbol of mourning for all our inhumanity.

Some questions to help your own imagining of this story:

1 What picture comes into your mind when you read the story?
2 What are some of the emotions you associate with the story?
3 Where do you see a similar kind of suffering through violence today?
4 Can you begin to imagine how you would respond to such an act of personal violence?
5 Where do you see God in the story?

6 What is one thing you can do to respond to this kind of suffering today?

Another passage in the Gospels which deals with a mother watching the death of her son is John 19.25-27, where Jesus gives Mary into the care of John. You might like to imagine this story, using the questions above to help you.

7. Jesus Visits Martha and Mary

'Martha was upset'
LUKE 10.38–42

As Jesus and his disciples went on their way, he came to a village where a woman named Martha welcomed him into her home. She had a sister named Mary who sat down at the feet of the Lord and listened to his teaching. Martha was upset over all the work she had to do, so she came and said, 'Lord, don't you care that my sister has left me to do all the work by myself. Tell her to come and help me!' The Lord answered her, 'Martha, Martha! You are worried and troubled over so many things, but just one is needed. Mary has chosen the right thing, and it will not be taken away from her.'

Martha MacDonald believed that the time for sitting down and talking was *after* the work was done. She also believed that if a thing was worth doing, it was worth doing well. This made her home a place of beauty and order, and everything in it was pleasing to the eye and relaxing to the spirit for the people who came to visit it. And there were many of them, because Martha was a hospitable woman, who loved to entertain, and spent many hours in the kitchen studying recipe books from all over the world and, as they say in the Southern States of America, 'cooking up a storm'.

Her younger sister, Mary, on the other hand, could sit in the midst of a tornado blowing through the house and never notice – or, to be more accurate, could let milk pans boil over, forget to put coal on the fire so that it died, get into a bed that had been untouched since she tumbled out of it that morning, and see a spider's web as the occasion for deep meditation on the nature of life, rather than as an evil which had to be furiously combated with dustpans and brushes. This was because she spent most of her waking hours (and some of the sleeping ones too) with her nose in a book. She read the newspaper from cover to cover while eating her toast in the morning, she read while waiting at the bus stop (and was hence often late for work), she bumped her head on lamp-posts that she walked into while trying to read and walk at the same time, she read in her lunch-hour and whenever nobody was watching at work, and at night-time she lay for hours in bed, wandering through all the worlds of the books she borrowed from libraries, bought at jumble sales and was lent by friends. Her infuriated sister would say to the rest of the family that Mary was a bookworm – she didn't read books, she ate them, and, indeed, she devoured them with the avidity of a starving man faced with a king's banquet. All this reading left her very little time to acquire other, more practical skills – she didn't know one end of a knitting needle from the other, her preference in cooking was for toasted cheese and packets of chocolate digestives which she would munch her way through without ever looking to see what she was eating, and she had been expressly forbidden to even attempt a simple task like changing a plug in case she blew them all to kingdom come.

This little personality difference between the two sisters

Jesus Visits Martha and Mary

naturally led to some tensions. Martha, who had shouldered the burdens of the household since their parents had died within six months of each other ten years before, often found herself in a state of fury with Mary's apparent unconcern for the way they lived, the fact that there were essential tasks that, just for survival, had to be performed, and the even more pressing fact that she seemed to be the only one in the house who noticed when these tasks required doing. Though she was a naturally cheerful and optimistic woman, she did feel that living with Mary was enough to try the patience of a saint, and she was certainly no saint. There were times when she felt more like a martyr, offering herself up on the altar of a house which everyone seemed to like, but no one else would take seriously.

As for Mary, there were moments when she surfaced for long enough from her books to be aware of Martha running around cleaning and cooking and washing, and to feel somewhat guilty at all this frenzy of activity happening around her. Sometimes she tried to get Martha to sit down and relax and read a book or something. But when she did that, either Martha would mutter furiously that not everyone could afford to take it easy when there was work to be done and would stomp around ostentatiously crashing dishes, or, if she sat down, she was so fidgety that Mary could tell that she was thinking about the kitchen cupboards that needed to be cleaned out, and how she could be catching up with the ironing. And sometimes, when she had these twinges of conscience, because she knew how hard Martha worked, what with her job at the surgery, and keeping the house going and entertaining lots of people, she tried to help. But she so often got things wrong, or was slow, or found Martha following her around doing it all again that she would eventually disappear, to be found an hour later, duster in hand, in her usual position curled up in an armchair, chewing her fingers and deep in Jane Austen or Agatha Christie or a newspaper article on the nomadic peoples of the Sahara – it didn't really matter which, because she read whatever she could lay her hands on. So Martha went on doing everything for her, and getting a little more shrewish every year, and Mary went on reading, and pretending not to notice. Every now and then, a storm would blow up, and Martha would lose her temper and shout vigorously and Mary would be penitent, and Martha would relent and Mary would promise to try harder, and they would be friends again, because they loved each other very much.

Then there was Laz. Laz was Martha and Mary's younger brother. He had been just ten years old when their parents died, and his sisters had brought him up, gently supporting him through the first awful months when a little boy eagerly looking forward to life had become a confused and unhappy and withdrawn child, encouraging him through the trials and tribulations of adolescence, and welcoming him into the world of adult companionship. These years had drawn them close, allies at times against a world which had lost its foundation, and against the watchful and inquisitive gaze of neighbours and relatives in their small town, who were not slow to question the wisdom of a young boy being raised by two girls barely out of their teens, and were too much in the habit of offering unwanted advice. And they took their responsibility seriously. Martha cooked his favourite meals for him, sometimes making do with eggs so that he could have chops. She got him up for school each morning, and sent him off with his packed lunch, and his gym kit neatly pressed. She baked for school coffee evenings, determined that he shouldn't suffer from being motherless, made house room for a trail of boys 'come to see Laz', and later, washed football strips, somehow found the money for school trips, and passed sharp comment on the giggly girls who wanted to talk to him on the phone at all hours. Mary, too, in her way, cared for this small boy with the captivating smile and ingenuous manner, who grew into serious adolescence and then passionate youth. She read him stories in the early days of loss, hours of escape for a sore hurt. She helped him with his homework, sometimes spending much time and effort educating herself in the mysteries of calculus and the further reaches of Latin poetry so that she could help him better. She was delighted for him when he got into university to study politics. And sometimes, when Martha wasn't watching, she would slip him money to go to the theatre or to entertain the latest girlfriend in style.

Jesus Visits Martha and Mary

Now Laz still lived at home travelling the ten miles into the city to university, and Martha still got him up for his lectures before she got Mary up to go to her civil service job and herself went to the surgery where she was a receptionist. She still did his washing, and she cooked supper and poured out beer for the stream of noisy, animated students, artists and eccentrics he brought home with him almost every day, assuring them of their welcome. And while they talked politics, argued about the causes of poverty and the value of religion, planned student campaigns and cursed the government, Mary sat with them, listening, a little envious of the freedom and excitement of their erratic lives in comparison with her own rather mundane existence and, occasionally, joined in, though she was sometimes aware of her own limitations with all these slightly younger people who seemed so sure of themselves and of their opinions. And Laz, loving, impetuous, cherished, idealistic, never really noticed how much work his friends gave Martha, nor wondered whether Mary's talents were really being used in her dull job. If he had, he would certainly have done something about it.

They might have gone on that way for a long time, Martha working and Mary reading and Laz trying to change the world, at least till Laz, as he probably would do, left home, or one of them got married. But something happened then which subtly and indefinably altered the balance of their relationship for ever. It was all to do with Laz's friend. He had many friends, and was always making more, but this one was somehow special.

Martha and Mary first heard about him when Laz came home one day and started, almost before he got in the door, talking about a man he'd heard speaking at some fringe meeting of the kind that always seemed to be happening round the university. No, he wasn't a student, he was a bit older than that, probably even as old as Martha. (Martha, who thought that at thirty-two she was just coming into the prime of life, took umbrage a bit at that.) No, he wasn't a lecturer, he spoke much better than most of the opinionated and verbose folk in *his* department anyway. Was he a politician? No, he wasn't, though a lot of what he said applied to politics, especially what he said about money, and the dignity of the poor. Was he a minister? No, he wasn't, though he seemed to have a very intimate relationship with God, and no embarrassment at all about talking about God, which was unusual these days, when the clergy either did everything they could to avoid mentioning such an unfashionable thing as faith, or nauseated you with their going on about AIDS and the moral law and made you feel that they were selling something. Was he famous, had he been on television, or written books? No, he hadn't, not that Laz knew, although he thought he was probably starting to get up a lot of people's noses with some of the things he was saying. And he did seem to have a lot of friends, though even his own liberal student friends had been a little shocked to see him in a pub with one of the city's most notorious con-merchants, talking to a girl who was a known slag. Not that they'd ever admit it, of course.

By this time, his sisters were definitely intrigued, though Martha was also a little apprehensive. But her hospitable heart got the better of her, and she told Laz to bring him home for a meal on Friday.

Friday wasn't a very auspicious day for Martha. It had been particularly busy at the surgery, with a lot of patients who complained and grumbled about the doctors, which she, of course, at the desk, bore the brunt of. By the time she got away in the evening, she was just too late to catch the shops, and it was only when she was sitting on the bus going home that she remembered that Laz was coming home with his friend for a meal. She hurriedly ran through the contents of the fridge and larder in her mind, slightly panicky because she didn't like to let her reputation as a great cook down, and resignedly settled on a cheese and egg pie, slittery to make because of the pastry, but she had the ingredients in the house, and Laz liked it. Then fruit salad. Her temper, however, was not helped when she got into the house and found Mary sitting there reading a new book, with the fire unlit, not even laid, and her wet coat draped over the sofa dripping on to the floor. Martha slammed the door, and rushed into the kitchen to turn on the oven. Thankfully, she at least had the fire lit when Laz and his friend appeared.

Martha was aware that she was fussing and flustered

while she brought them in and took their coats, and she hated that. She liked to be organized and to have everything under control. But she did her best to be polite to Laz's friend, who certainly looked nice enough, and not at all as if he was bothered by his slightly less than enthusiastic reception. He just said hello, and smiled, and went and sat down beside the fire. She sat for a couple of minutes making polite conversation, and asking him about himself and what he did, without really taking in the answers, then, irritably aware of the pie still needing to be made, she excused herself and went into the kitchen. From there, as she chopped and rolled and trimmed and peeled, she could hear the other three in the living-room, talking and laughing, and she stabbed savagely into an onion. Just tonight, she would have liked to stay with them, talking and laughing and getting to know Laz's nice friend a bit better. Just for once, she'd have liked to put down the burden of responsibility for the endless load of people to feed, and clothes to wash, and rooms to clean, and be carefree and listen and put in her little bit. She had things to say, didn't she? She had thoughts, didn't she, about life and the world and the government and religion? Just for once, she was fed up being the one who made it happen for everybody else. Tonight, she wanted it to happen for her. As the conversation next door became more animated, her knife sliced and cut and spun with increasing fury. At last, she could bear it no longer.

She stalked to the kitchen door and opened it. The others looked up and saw her standing in the doorway, and the talk died. She looked at the three of them, Laz, long and lanky, stretched out in the armchair on one side of the fire. Laz's friend sitting back in the other, looking at her. And Mary, deposed from her armchair, sitting on the rug, hugging her knees, looking up at this man, her face alive with happiness. As she looked at them, they seemed to form a circle in the firelight, while she was excluded, out here in the darkness of the fluorescent light of the kitchen. She felt shut out, hurt, pushed to the edge.

The other three could tell that Martha was upset. You'd have needed to be a robot not to realize it, it emanated from her in waves. Laz had a look of consternation on his face.

Mary assumed her usual guilty expression. Laz's friend just looked at her, waiting. The years of frustration with Mary, the years of caring for Laz rendered her incapable of expressing her feelings to them. She looked at the man who was new, who seemed as if he might understand. 'Please sir', she said, 'please sir, don't you care that my sister's left me to do all the work by myself? Tell her to come and help me.' The surprise of hearing the normally capable Martha addressing his friend as 'sir' left Laz silent. Mary, hearing the pain in Martha's voice, started to get up. But the man put his hand lightly on Mary's shoulder, and she sat down again. Then he got up and went over to Martha, standing in the doorway, and put his arm round her shoulder and drew her over to the fireside. He sat her down in the chair he'd just been in, and sat down on the floor beside her.

'Poor Martha', he said, 'so many things to worry about. Mary's fine where she is, let's just leave her there. But you, you need to come and sit down too, because we're all missing your conversation. Never mind about the dinner. Laz can go out in a minute and get fish and chips and we'll just eat it sitting round the fire like this. Laz told me all about his sisters, and I was really looking forward to meeting you both. I don't want you wearing yourself out for me. I'm happy with anything. It's quite enough that you've made me welcome in your house – there's a lot of folk wouldn't even let me over the doorstep. What matters is that you're here, and that we can talk.'

It was a long time since Martha had had anyone expressing that kind of concern for her. Not since her parents died, that she could remember. The feeling with this man that she didn't have to do anything, or prove anything, or be responsible for him felt like a great weight lifting off her shoulders, and the tension drained out of her, so that she felt suddenly at peace. She liked this friend of Laz's. She liked all his friends, but most of them seemed to enjoy her cooking without being unduly interested in what, if anything, she had to say. And they did tend to make her feel old and a little spinsterish. This man made her feel young.

Mary and Laz watched in amazement as their sister, who they couldn't remember ever having sat still for more than

Jesus Visits Martha and Mary

half an hour, visibly unwound before their eyes, and seemed to open out like a flower that had been tightly closed in on itself. Their conversation that night flowed, they ate fish and chips with much merriment out of newspapers, and drank some red wine, and they sat till the embers were almost dark in the fireplace. They talked about Laz's dreams of helping the poor to get justice, and about Mary's love of books which had so often been seen either as a strange aberration for a small-town girl, or simply as a waste of time, and they discovered that Laz's friend had a great knowledge of his country's history and religion, and a poet's feeling for words. And Mary and Laz realized that their sister's practical wisdom and sense of the importance of things that had seemed trivial to them, things like making people feel welcome by preparing food and a pleasant atmosphere for them, and like being responsible with money, and the fact that she knew by name every shopkeeper in the town and all the neighbouring children, that all these were actually admired and valued by their friend. They suddenly began to realize that there were dimensions of life they were missing out on, that Martha knew about, by her involvement in these day-to-day cares. And Martha – well, Martha talked, and talked, and talked. About what mattered to *her*, about what *her* hopes and dreams were, and about a whole lot of inconsequential stuff they none of them could remember later, but which they knew had made them laugh, and cry, and get excited, and be silent. They couldn't explain why, or what it was, but all three of them knew that that was the night when things changed. After that night, they spent more time with him, and Mary started to talk about possibly going to university to study theology, and Martha stopped trying to carry the world on her back and found that, surprisingly, it didn't drop. She got better at doing nothing, and just being. And Mary began to notice more of the things that needed to be done around the place, though she never stopped automatically reading the information on the cornflakes packet. The house didn't look any worse to anyone who came into it, though sometimes Martha would get an itch to go and clean the bath again after someone came out of it – an itch she just sat on. Mary never did learn to knit, or to change a plug.

And as for Laz and his friend. Well, that's another story.

* * *

I have loved this story for a long time: for the encouragement Jesus gave to Mary which broke a convention that a woman's primary function was as a servant; for its portrayal of a very real domestic situation; but most of all for its kindness. Jesus, in affirming Mary's right to listen and learn, was kind to the flustered Martha, who, after all, was only doing what she had been brought up to think of as her duty. It is a tremendously encouraging story for women. In Jewish society, they were forbidden to learn the Torah, the Law, and had no independent religious identity, only what they received as daughters, as wives, as sisters. In this incident, Jesus gave to Mary the chance to listen and learn and think in her own right. Perhaps it is also a challenging story for men: in drawing Martha out of the kitchen, Jesus must have been prepared for the fact that the cost of women's participation in a religious life of their own might be a less comprehensive domestic service – or, at least in our society, one in which men might play their part. And it's a challenging story for us all, as we try to discern what is right and appropriate in each situation.

Some questions to help your own imagining of this story:

1 What do *you* do to welcome a guest into your home?
2 Whose welcome do you identify with more, Martha's or Mary's?
3 Where, in your life, can you see too much busyness that prevents you from listening?
4 Jesus helped Martha to stop being busy. What help do you need?
or:
Is there someone close to you who needs your help to stop being too busy?

Two passages you might like to imagine which have some bearing on the story of Mary and Martha are the story of the Good Samaritan (Luke 10.25-37) and the story of Jesus washing the feet of his disciples (John 13.1-17).

The first of these, which immediately precedes the story

Jesus Visits Martha and Mary

of Mary and Martha, makes it clear that Jesus does not in any way dismiss or undervalue practical service and care. Rather, he stresses the importance of responding appropriately, and in this situation it is action rather than contemplation which is called for. This is also a story which examples kindness as a fundamental quality of neighbourly love.

The second of these stories is one in which Jesus, once again defying convention, washes the dirty feet of his friends, thereby taking upon himself a duty which was always performed by a woman or a slave. This act of humility would be confusing to the disciples, for whom humility was a despised sign of weakness. Imagine you are one of the disciples.

8. The Woman Caught in Adultery

'They all left, one by one, the older ones first'
JOHN 8.1-11

Then everyone went home, but Jesus went to the Mount of Olives. Early the next morning he went back to the Temple. All the people gathered round him, and he sat down and began to teach them. The teachers of the Law and the Pharisees brought in a woman who had been caught committing adultery, and they made her stand before them all. 'Teacher', they said to Jesus, 'This woman was caught in the very act of committing adultery. In our Law, Moses commanded that such a woman must be stoned to death. Now, what do you say?' They said this to trap Jesus, so that they could accuse him.

But he bent over and wrote on the ground with his finger. As they stood there asking him questions, he straightened himself up and said to them, 'Whichever of you has committed no sin may throw the first stone at her.' Then he bent over again and wrote on the ground. When they heard this, they all left, one by one, the older ones first. Jesus was left alone, with the woman still standing there. He straightened himself up and said to her, 'Where are they? Is there no one left to condemn you?'

'No one, sir', she answered.

'Well, then', Jesus said, 'I do not condemn you either. Go, but do not sin again.'

I knew something was going to happen that morning. There was too much anger, too much outrage, too many people feeling their position threatened for it not to spill out and catch fire eventually. Never before in the life of our church had there been such trouble. People in corners whispering to each other, saying things behind each other's backs, opposing groups forming, and none of it ever coming out into the open. I suppose we had got comfortable, set in our ways, nothing much ever to disturb our peaceful waters, nothing worse than worrying about falling numbers on a Sunday morning, and the cost of a new church roof. Then it seemed to hit us all at once.

First of all, there was the scandal of Ruth Andrews. Ruth and her husband were leading members of the church; he was an elder, convener of the property committee, in business for himself, successful, well-respected; Ruth was a Sunday School teacher, sang in the choir, had been vice-president of the Young Women's Group. She was one of the liveliest women in the church – friendly, outgoing, vivacious, always ready with a song at church socials, the first to volunteer if something needed to be done. They had two kids, and seemed for all the world like your perfect family. That's why it was such a shock for people when the tongues started wagging. There are a lot of women you wouldn't have been surprised to hear it about, but Ruth – a pillar of the church, good husband, no financial worries. People in the church were outraged.

She was having an affair with another man. He wasn't a member of the church. He wasn't a member of any church. In fact, nobody could understand what she saw in him. For a start, he was younger than she was. She must have been in her mid-thirties, and he must have been nearly ten years younger. He didn't appear to have a job, said he was an 'artist', whatever that means. He was long-haired, scruffy, and had a pretty questionable lifestyle. He wore a leather jacket! People were disgusted. It wasn't so bad at first, when they seemed to be just friends – although even then, people didn't approve of her choice of friends. But then she started to get careless about where and when she met him. They were seen together sitting in her car, and once, holding hands in the street. One day, someone saw her leaving his flat in the small hours of the morning, and after that there was no holding the gossip. She began to look strained and unhappy, and to avoid seeing people from the church. She and her husband still came to church on a Sunday – no one knew how much he knew or suspected, and he wasn't the kind of man you could ask – and she still sang in the choir and taught in the Sunday School. That outraged people even further. How dare she come around among respectable people? She should have the decency to stay away. How did she have the nerve to go on teaching in the Sunday School, corrupting the children? The rumours, the talk, had been building up for months now, and I didn't see how it could go on any longer without something happening. Perhaps that day.

And as if that wasn't enough, there was all the business with the new preacher who had turned up. This was a young man who came from somewhere up north, and though he wasn't a minister, he must have had some kind of training, because he certainly knew his Bible, and there was no doubt that he knew how to hold a congregation when he was preaching. It wasn't your fire-and-brimstone kind of preaching, nor the dreary little homilies you get in some churches. It wasn't even the kind we were more used to in our church, going through the Scriptures verse by verse, and trying to make some sense of a language that most of us couldn't understand very well. No, this man was very down-to-earth, he didn't argue or shout or make loud speeches. He just spoke quite gently, telling a lot of stories about everyday things, using words that everyone could understand, even the old dears and the young kids. The teenagers liked him, and had stopped grumbling so much

The Woman Caught in Adultery

about coming to church since he started preaching, and quite a lot of new people were there on Sunday mornings now. Some of them were friends that came with him, and then some others who had just drifted in. Some of them were pretty unlikely too. There were some soldiers from the barracks up the road. Well, that was all right, at least they were soldiers, although they weren't popular in the area, with so many of them being stationed here from overseas. It's just that they never usually came to church. But there were a few distinctly shady characters, ex-cons, swindlers and people like that, who seemed to have come under this young fellow's influence. They tended to dress rather loudly and wear too much after-shave for folk's liking, and it was hard for the members to take their apparent change of heart at face value. We kept expecting the communion plate to have disappeared one Sunday, and them along with it.

Then there were quite a lot of young, student types, the kind that are always up in arms about the state of the world, always going on marches and getting up petitions. There had already been some heated arguments between some of them and some of the congregation about money, and the state of the country – and this is a congregation that has several men in high places in it! And there were folk who came from the housing scheme down the road, who obviously had no idea of how to behave in the church, and upset some of the old folk because they let their children run up and down the aisles during the service. Some of them were obviously quite hard up, and the church didn't always smell very nice on a Sunday morning. And some of the women were quite brassy. But it's probably not fair to blame the smell on them. It mostly came from the tramps. At least, they were what we used to call tramps – dirty old men, and one woman, who obviously slept rough and stank of drink and carried plastic bags that they wouldn't let the elders put in the cloakroom when they came into church.

All this had got the elders into a right state. They didn't know how to cope with what was going on. On the one hand the preacher certainly brought a lot of new people into the church, and livened up some of the sleeping members. The children loved him, he was popular with the young folk, and his preaching *was* good. But on the other hand, quite a few of the elders weren't sure if these new folk were the kind we wanted in our church, they didn't seem to fit in. He had upset some people with some of his preaching, especially the stuff about money, and about not thinking yourself better than others. The minister wasn't very happy about his theology, which he said was unorthodox to say the least, and though he had a strong influence on the young people, we didn't know if that was altogether a good thing. Already a number of parents were worried in case their children took it into their heads to give up their steady jobs and go off to do voluntary work with deprived kids or, worse, to become too religious. Some of them were already talking about prayer and God more than seemed normal for their age, and it did tend to make the parents uncomfortable.

Their fears had not been lessened by a story someone heard about an incident that had taken place when the young man had been staying in a town on his way down from the north, when he had encouraged another young man who was very well-off, with a good job, and highly thought of in his church, to sell all his possessions, give the money to charity and come with him. Though the young chap hadn't done it, it had alarmed some of our members a lot when they heard about it.

A few of the elders, the ones who had been keen that he be allowed to preach in the first place, were all in favour of him. But the minister and the majority of the elders felt it was all rather risky, that they might drive away some of the best givers in the congregation, and that this young man, with his orthodoxy in doubt, was in danger of undermining their authority in the church. I think myself that they had already decided what was going to happen that Sunday, that they set him up so that they could catch him out in a way that would give them the excuse to get rid of him once and for all. Oh yes, I knew something was going to happen that morning, both with Ruth and with the preacher. It just didn't turn out quite the way anyone expected it to.

The church was packed, both with regular members, many of whom knew something was up, and with a lot of the new folk, who all seemed quite cheerful and un-

The Woman Caught in Adultery

concerned. There was the usual buzz of people greeting their neighbours, shuffling along pews, children dropping their offerings, hymn books rustling. Then Ruth Andrews and her husband came in. Immediately, a silence fell. They must have noticed it, and she shivered as if she was cold, but they took their places and the service began. The atmosphere was tense, but when the young man began preaching, you could see a lot of folk beginning to relax. At the end of the service, the organist was just about to strike up with the recessional, when the minister came forward and held up his hand for silence. Immediately, everyone stopped gathering their bits and pieces, and listened intently as he announced that there would be a special meeting of all elders and office-bearers straight away, requesting that as many as possible attend, as they had a matter of the 'utmost gravity' for the church to deal with. Then he sat down.

The congregation began to leave the church, talking excitedly, leaving about fifty men scattered throughout the church. I was one of them. Though I am not an elder, I have always been happy to put my skills as a tradesman at the service of the church, and I had been elected to the congregational board several times. When I was younger and fitter, I had trained the boys' football team. So I had stayed in my seat, and after one glance at me, my wife got up and went out. I knew that she would be burning with curiosity when I went home. I looked around the church at these men, most of whom I knew well, ordinary, decent men, mostly middle-aged, some older, a few young ones. I noticed that Tom Andrews had gone.

The minister stood up again, and called us to the front, where we all stood around uncomfortably. 'I've asked our preacher to wait', he said. The young man was sitting in one of the seats reserved for the choir. He had taken out a notebook and a pen, and they lay on his knee.

Then the church door opened, and two of the elders came in with Ruth Andrews. They must have stopped her as she left the church. As they walked up the aisle towards us, I could see that she was very white. They directed her on to the chancel steps, to where she was standing right in front of the young man, with all the rest of us looking on. She was shaking with nerves. I thought then, this is it, she's in at the deep end now. And she must have known that too.

The minister spoke to the preacher. 'Now, my friend', he said. 'This woman, a member of this church, has been caught having an affair with a man. She is a married woman with children, she is a member of the choir, she is a teacher in the Sunday School. Apart altogether from the hurt this liaison must be causing her husband and children, apart from the scandal that this has caused in the community and the disrepute into which this church has been brought, and never mind the fact that people do not want their children taught by someone who presents such a bad example to them – apart from all these things, the fact is that this woman has clearly broken the law of God, which says, 'Thou shalt not commit adultery'. There's no question but that they are lovers, people have seen them, and she has admitted as much. The teaching of this church is that she has broken the commandments, the law of God. I think we have to make an example of her. Our society is becoming more and more permissive, and its moral values are being corrupted. There is no respect for the family left, and you know where that is leading us – to promiscuity, to the breakdown of marriage, to the evil of one-parent families, to disease and immorality. If the church doesn't take a stand against this sort of thing, who will? We cannot allow this situation to go on any longer. We must speak clearly in condemnation of adultery. We must let our congregation understand that this kind of behaviour will not be countenanced. Mrs Andrews must be asked to resign from her membership of the choir, from her teaching in the Sunday School and from her membership of this church. What is your view?'

I looked at the men around me. I could see that there were many who were nodding in agreement with the minister. I knew them well enough to read the unspoken words in their eyes. 'How could you do something like this to a good bloke like Tom?' – that was a friend of his. 'What did you see in a young punk like that?' – this from men who were deeply suspicious of a kind of manhood very different from theirs. 'Did you never consider the scandal?' – from a highly-placed civil servant, aware of the power of the gutter press. 'What

The Woman Caught in Adultery

kind of a mother are you, anyway?' – from a young man whose own family were the light of his life. 'We mustn't tolerate this kind of immorality in the church' – from a serious young man who ran the Bible Class. Oh yes, there were many there who were quite ready to pin a scarlet letter on her, men who were indignant, outraged, worst of all, betrayed by one of their own.

I looked at Ruth. She had gone ashen now. I realized that she too was imagining the words being spoken, she too could feel the looks of disgust being thrown at her. I knew that they would hit her with the force of stones being hurled, that the looks of contempt pierced her to the bone. The church had been such a big part of her life. She had given it her time and commitment, and these had been her friends. She really believed. I thought that she must be wretched, feeling the guilt of how she had hurt her husband, her children. Who knows what had made her do what she had done? But it was clear from looking at her that to be thrown out of the church, which was so important to her, to be publicly stripped of her duties within it, would be like a death sentence to her, the death of her spirit.

I looked at the minister and elders who had arranged this confrontation. You had to hand it to them, they were clever. They had the preacher trapped, caught between the devil and the deep blue sea. If he rejected the suggestion of the elders, that the woman be condemned and sentenced, they could accuse him of flouting the law of God, of appearing to condone immorality, of flying in the face of all that the church had taught, and held sacred, over generations. Then they would be free to say that his theology was wrong, his teaching suspect, his influence bad, then they could silence him, and undermine his authority with the people. I did not see how he could go that way. Though I had some sympathy for Ruth, and did not like the way she was being used by these men, I too believed that the breaking of faith in marriage was wrong, and should not be treated as if it were a thing of no consequence. A promise is a promise, and if betrayal of promises was seen as the norm, then there would soon be no honour anywhere. I could not respect a preacher who took such a breach of trust lightly.

But if he accepted their judgement, then he would be

party to an awful thing, to a kind of death. For all that I believed in the upholding of trust and loyalty I could not see that this was the best way to go about it. And there would be many in the community, perhaps even in the church, who would feel the same way. They would see such a judgement, such a punishment, as savage, barbaric even. From what I had seen and heard of the young man, his gentleness, his understanding of the problems facing ordinary people, his compassion for human weakness, I could not see him aligning himself with the hardness of this condemnation. Truly, he was trapped. I looked at the preacher. He had not said a word all the time the minister was speaking. He hardly seemed to be paying attention, as the elders joined in a chorus of questions, asking him for his decision. He just sat there, writing something in his notebook. Then he straightened himself up, and looked round at them. And said, 'Whichever one of you has never done anything wrong can be the first to condemn her.' Then he bent down and started writing in his notebook again. There was a stunned silence. It was not what they had expected. No one spoke, no one moved. you could see the embarrassment begin to spread across many faces, as the full force of what he had said struck them. There wasn't one of us who could claim to have led completely blameless lives. I certainly couldn't. I remembered an incident of many years ago, with a secretary in the office. Oh, it hadn't amounted to anything, really, but only because the girl had been more sensible than I. And I thought of some of the things I didn't really like to think of, times when I'd bent the rules, if not broken them, times when I'd got drunk and regretted it later, words I'd said in anger. No, I could not be the first to accuse her. From the way we all avoided each other's eyes, you could see we were all remembering things we'd rather not. Still, no one spoke. Then Jim Donaldson turned round, and walked out of the church. He was one of the senior elders, a quiet, honest, kind man. Then another man followed him, and another, and another. They were mostly older men. Maybe we older men had had more time and opportunity to do wrong – I knew some of these men had been through the war, and had discovered things about themselves then that they didn't like. Maybe life had taught

The Woman Caught in Adultery

us to be a little more tolerant of the weaknesses of others. Maybe we didn't mind losing face as much as the younger ones. I don't know. I've sometimes thought that young people have a greater tendency to see life as much more black and white, right or wrong, without being aware of the huge grey patches that are what the rest of us experience. This can be a good thing sometimes, gives them strong ideals, but it can also make them very intolerant, especially of the failings of their elders. Anyway, the older men left first, and me with them.

The others went out, and went away, not speaking to each other, all of them deep in their own thoughts and memories. But I have to confess that I hung around in the church porch, out of sight, but from where I could still see what was happening in the church. One of the preacher's friends was there, a young fellow called John. He had obviously been nervous about leaving him alone, and had stayed when the rest of the congregation left. I watched the minister come out, and walk past me without speaking, his face set. Only the young men were still there. Then one by one they left too, until finally only Ruth and the preacher were still in the church. It was wrong of me, I suppose, but I wanted to see what would happen then.

I saw that he looked up from whatever it was he was still writing in his notebook. He looked at her, standing there, with a mixture of relief and hope and fear on her face. Then he said to her, 'Where have they all gone? Is there no one still here to condemn you?'

'No', she said, timidly.

'Well then', the preacher said. 'I don't condemn you either. Go on, now – but don't do such a wrong thing again.'

I loved that man, then. I saw the light come back into Ruth's eyes, as if she believed once more that she had a future, that there could somehow be a new beginning for her, that once again she had the power to choose how her life would be, instead of simply being driven by so many conflicting feelings. She walked out of the church with dignity. I always did have a soft spot for her, for her liveliness and warmth, and in the end I'd rather have someone with passion, even if it sometimes got them into trouble, than one of your cold, correct, loveless folk. But I reckon that the preacher made some enemies that day. He made us look at ourselves, and judge ourselves before we stood in judgement of someone else, and we didn't like what we saw. When you see yourself as you are, you have the choice to remember it, and let it make you a bit kinder, a bit less ready to jump in and howl for blood. I hope I have the courage to make that choice. But some folk just want to get the person who brought them face to face with themselves, and make sure he never has the chance to do it again. I don't know what'll happen to the preacher now. But I'll be there this Sunday to find out. I have a personal interest in him now.

* * *

This story is an age-old one, the unfaithful wife and the outraged community. And it seems wise in human understanding – the fact that it is specifically mentioned that the older ones in the crowd left first suggests that with age comes a greater ability to admit to one's own experience, and a tendency to be a little less judgemental. It also reflects the tendency of the young to see things in a much more black-and-white fashion, and sometimes to be puritanically unmerciful, not just with sexual weakness, but with all the failings of their elders. Jesus, in rejecting the death of the woman, and challenging her accusers to reflect on their own sin, simply faced them with the opportunity to be honest with themselves. And he would not allow them to shift the responsibility for what was to happen to the woman on to him, and so to be absolved for their involvement in the human condition. He made them play the role, not just of accuser, but of judge and defender.

But as well as being a story about morality and forgiveness, this is also an important scene in the ongoing drama of Jesus' confrontation with the authorities. When we read this story, it is easy to see the suggested stoning as a barbaric act of mob violence, one which would be unthinkable in our society. But in fact, stoning to death was the legitimately ordained punishment for adultery in Jesus' society. The Pharisees were trying to trap Jesus, to force him either to break the Jewish law and speak against the punishment, or to accept the punishment and a cruel and unloving death. Jesus would not be caught, however. He

The Woman Caught in Adultery

turned the trap back on his questioners and challenged them to personal responsibility.

In trying to imagine how this story would happen today, I found that I could not simply move it forward in time, but had to try to reinterpret the event while remaining true to its original meaning and intention. The notion of a woman being stoned to death for adultery I found just too alien to imagine happening in our society. And furthermore, since we live in a country where there is separation of church and state, we do not attempt to legislate against adultery, which is seen as a personal, moral issue. The only legislation we have in this country deals with the possible consequences of adultery (family breakdown, property disputes and so on). And though our society may pay lip-service to its disapproval of such an action, in reality, much of media coverage, and our public discussion tends to portray adultery as something which is glamorous, exciting and at least understandable. I wanted to imagine a situation where this was seen as a real crime, not just against God but against the community, and where the penalty for the crime would be a painful and deeply felt one.

Therefore, I found that for me, the choice was between imagining the story happening in a fundamentalist Islamic state, where such punishments still do happen, or imagining it in the context where the punishment, though not a literal death, would, in its humiliation, rejection and despair, feel like a death of the spirit. Since I did not feel I know enough about Islamic countries, their values, religion and customs, I chose the latter context.

Some questions to help your own imagining of this story:
1 Whom do you most identify with in the story?
2 What is it about that person that you identify with in particular?
3 Is there a situation in your life where you are judging without also being prepared to judge your own actions?
4 Jesus would not enforce the law of stoning. Are there any laws in our society that you would have difficulty in enforcing – in the state, in the church?
5 Are there instances in which you have tried to force someone else to make your decision for you?

Another passage in Matthew's Gospel (Matthew 22.15-22), where the Pharisees tried to trap Jesus into choosing between the civil authorities and the Jewish law, tells how they asked him whether they should pay taxes to the Roman Emperor. You might like to imagine this story happening today, perhaps by asking Jesus about whether or not to pay an unpopular tax. How might Jesus answer that, and what would the circumstances be?

9. Jesus at the Home of Simon the Pharisee

'Whoever has been forgiven little shows only a little love'
LUKE 7.36–50

A Pharisee invited Jesus to have dinner with him, and Jesus went to his house and sat down to eat. In that town was a woman who lived a sinful life. She heard that Jesus was eating in the Pharisee's house, so she brought an alabaster jar full of perfume and stood behind Jesus, crying and wetting his feet with her tears. Then she dried his feet with her hair, kissed them, and poured the perfume on them. When the Pharisee saw this, he said to himself, 'If this man really were a prophet, he would know who this woman is who is touching him; he would know what kind of sinful life she lives.'

Jesus spoke up and said to him, 'Simon, I have something to tell you.'

'Yes, Teacher,' he said, 'tell me.'

'There were two men who owed money to a money-lender,' Jesus began. 'One owed him five hundred silver coins, and the other one fifty. Neither of them could pay him back, so he cancelled the debts of both. Which one, then, will love him more?'

'I suppose,' answered Simon, 'that it would be the one who was forgiven more.'

'You are right,' said Jesus. Then he turned to the woman and said to Simon, 'Do you see this woman? I came into your home, and you gave me no water for my feet, but she has washed my feet with her tears and dried them with her hair. You did not welcome me with a kiss, but she has not stopped kissing my feet since I came. You provided no olive-oil for my head, but she has covered my feet with perfume. I tell you, then, the great love she has shown proves that her many sins have been forgiven. But whoever has been forgiven little shows only a little love.'

Then Jesus said to the woman, 'Your sins are forgiven.'

The others sitting at the table began to say to themselves, 'Who is this, who even forgives sins?'

But Jesus said to the woman, 'Your faith has saved you; go in peace.'

It had been one of the most embarrassing evenings of Simon's life. If he had anticipated just how embarrassing, he doubted whether he would have invited the stranger to dinner. But he had thought that it might prove to be an interesting interlude in a life that had lately felt a little jaded; something to reminisce and laugh over with his friends sometime in the future ('Do you remember the night that Simon asked that strange young radical preacher to dinner, the one who made friends with all the tarts and cons in the district? Do you remember how all the bishops got their cassocks in a twist over him, and he upset the politicos? Said he was a subversive, or some such nonsense. Could have told you it was all a storm in a teacup – takes more than some lefty religious freak to upset our applecart, eh? And old Simon asked a few of us round, got out the claret and laid on a spread – wanted to see if the chap knew which knife and fork to use, see if he knew which end was up. Had a good laugh that night, didn't we, Si?').

And besides, he had been curious. It wasn't often the

Jesus at the Home of Simon the Pharisee

parson got in such a state about things, usually a placid old boy you could rely upon to do the needful in the pulpit, and keep the ladies happy. But a few Sundays ago, when he had turned up to do his bit with the lesson (he always went, believed church was a good thing, important for the fabric of society) here was the parson all agitated about a young fellow who had come to town just recently, having *walked* down from somewhere up North, would you believe, with a lot of weirdo friends, and was going around preaching about a new order, and having a bad influence on impressionable young people. Simon himself was inclined to take the parson's fulminations with a pinch of salt. He'd heard a lot of revolutionaries and holy-rollers in his time, and had discovered that usually one of two things happened to them. Either they deserted the great god Marx or the great god God for the even greater god Mammon, or they became so fanatical that even their closest followers began to feel the heat, and ran for cover. If it wasn't that, then it was some sordid little affair with a secretary. That had been his experience, though the combination of revolutionary and holy-roller was a new one on him. But a few quiet words in a few ears had elicited the information that this one seemed a little different. He didn't go about ranting and raving, and the people who had actually met him seemed to have gained quite a good impression, said he didn't make you cringe in the usual way. He had to admit that he was intrigued. Not that he thought the young man would seriously make any impact. Nobody really wanted the church to change; it was much too comfortable, and preachers were deluding themselves if they thought that anything other than money and vested interests had any power to change the social order. He should know, he had plenty of vested interests himself. Oh yes, he had a lifetime's experience in playing the power game, in playing the part of successful businessman, good family man, local dignitary and upright church member, always reliable for a hefty contribution to the steeple fund or the latest famine appeal. He knew about power, and if he sometimes found the interminable money talk of the men who were his friends unbearably tedious, or the strain of the part he played so well a little meaningless, he didn't let it bother him, because there was always the adrenalin of the next deal, next the decision, the next carefully-calculated gamble.

So he went out of his way to find the young man, and invite him for dinner, which he did with his usual impeccable charm and humour. If the young man was surprised to receive such an invitation, he didn't show it, but accepted quietly and politely. Simon was a little disappointed that he seemed so ordinary, nothing unusual about his appearance or dress or manner, and was half-inclined to think that he might have made a mistake, that they might all be in for a boring evening with a serious young man who would want to talk about the Bible all night, and ask them if they'd all been saved. In the event, he would have preferred an evening like that to what did in fact happen.

The evening started uneventfully. The young man arrived, still dressed in the same casual clothes, but Simon had been expecting that, hadn't imagined that he would carry a lounge suit around with him in his backpack or whatever it was he carried his possessions in. Simon had introduced his friends, and they'd all gone in to dinner. The conversation round the table was uninspiring to say the least. The young man seemed to be waiting for them to take the initiative, and though one or two of his friends had tried to get him going, even been a little provocative, his guest had been non-committal in his replies. Mrs Hobbs had served the meal (his wife had gone up to town to visit their daughter, declaring that she was having nothing to do with this odd whim of her husband's) and they had reached the coffee and brandy. Some of his friends had drunk a lot of wine, and Simon hoped wearily that they weren't going to get going on the slightly blue, slightly racist jokes that they seemed to find so entertaining. They had just pushed their chairs back to move to the other room for their coffee when the door flew open, and a woman came in, with Mrs Hobbs fluttering after her, apologizing and arguing with the woman at the same time.

The woman knew exactly who she was looking for. She made straight for the young man, and, as all the others watched with amazement, she dropped to her knees beside him, and burst into tears.

Jesus at the Home of Simon the Pharisee

For a moment, the whole room was silent, apart from the sound of the woman's sobbing. Simon looked at her. She was young, quite pretty, smartly dressed. He realized that he knew her. It was, after all, a small town. She was a woman one sometimes saw in hotel bars, occasionally on her own, more often with a man – not the same man. She was a woman who had something of a reputation for being an easy pick-up. Not quite on the bottom rung of the prostitution ladder, not the 'five pounds and I'll give you a good time in the back of your car' elderly whores who hung around the station and the harbour, but a little more classy than that. A comforter of travelling salesmen, a solace for abandoned husbands, the spice in the pot for bored executives. Oh yes, definitely a touch of class there; everyone knew her. She was the subject of many risqué jokes, the promise of escape, never taken, for some of his own friends (well, if my wife leaves me, there's always Mandy. . .).

He knew her, had occasionally wondered about her, what her story was. But he did not like her in his dining-room, making a spectacle of herself. She was kissing the young man's hands now, stroking them, and pressing them to her face. And the tears were running down her face, soaking the young man's hands. His guests all looked acutely embarrassed. A couple of them got up and wandered tactfully off into the sitting-room. Someone muttered something about hysterical women. Another offered to phone a doctor. Simon looked at the young man. He was the only one of them who still appeared quite at ease. He was gazing down at the woman, with a curious expression on his face.

Then the woman started to untie the young man's laces and to take off his boots. He was wearing a pair of ordinary work boots, somewhat muddy and battered. As they watched, she pulled them off, and pulled his socks off. Simon could not believe his eyes. From somewhere she produced a small bottle of what looked like massage oil, poured a little of it into the palms of her hands, and began to gently rub his feet. Her cheeks were stained with tears, but she had stopped crying, and she was looking up at the young man with a smile. She looked very young and very beautiful. She looked as he had sometimes seen women look when they held a baby in their arms – as if they held something so precious that they could not believe it. He realized that it was the rapt expression of the worshipper. He also realized that she was quite oblivious to the roomful of men staring at her, and to the highly-charged atmosphere she had created. They gazed with fascination at her, rubbing oil into a pair of sweaty, blistered feet with an almost voyeuristic attention. The contradiction between what he knew and had imagined of this woman and her bottle of oil, and the curiously innocent expression on her face was too acute for him to bear. He had to break the silence. 'Do you know who this woman is?' he almost shouted at the young man. 'What kind of preacher are you, if you let a whore like her fawn all over you?'

Simon didn't like to shout, it wasn't his style, but he was shouting now. And he was shaking. He couldn't understand what it was about all of this which was disturbing him so much. The scene was, of course, embarrassing and queer, but he had found himself in embarrassing situations before and coped with them with his own particular brand of detachment and calm. Was it because the woman was a prostitute? He couldn't see how. Though he knew that many of the men of his acquaintance were more familiar with women of her kind than they would ever care to admit, he himself had never been remotely tempted in that way – it would have seemed too squalid, too contemptible for his liking. He could too easily imagine the eyes of a woman who slept with unknown men for money, with no choice, no desire, no liking. The loathing, the knowing laughter, or simply the unutterable boredom. And behind that, the fear, the anxiety, the self-disgust. That had never been for him – he had too much pride. Then why should what he saw on a woman's face, when she was that kind of woman, disturb him?

Or was it that the young man was getting to him in some way? He had said very little, made no dramatic gestures, and yet Simon felt himself being observed. He did not like being looked at so closely, he preferred to be the one doing the watching. And it was ridiculous. He was not susceptible to romantic religious impulses, he liked a religion in which

Jesus at the Home of Simon the Pharisee

rules were clearly laid out. Then, without too much effort, too much thought, one could obey them, play one's expected role, and gain the rewards for right conduct. And the worldly rewards for right conduct were there to be seen – authority, being perceived as trustworthy, the protective mantle of respectability. As for the spiritual rewards – well, he tended to assume these without concerning himself over much with them. If you started to think too much about the thin line between an individual life and the vast eternity of the universe, too much about pain and suffering and the vulnerability of passion, too much about the dark places in the mind, it had the power to paralyse you, to reduce you to insignificance. Far better to play it by the rules and trust to their efficacy. So why was he suddenly so disturbed by a hysterical woman and a quiet man? He wasn't looking for a prophet or a saviour, merely for an interesting evening. What difference did it make to him that the young man had no powers of discrimination? He wasn't looking for anything, so he had no reason for disappointment.

Then the young man spoke for the first time. He spoke with unexpected authority. He did not attempt to apologize, to justify, to explain. He looked directly at Simon, and said to him, 'Simon, I have something to tell you.'

'Go on', said Simon sharply.

'There were two men who had both got badly into debt', the young man said. 'One of them owed £2000 and the other owed about £20,000. The friend from whom they had both borrowed the money realized that it would ruin both of them to pay him back, so he cancelled both the debts. Which one of these men would feel most grateful?'

Simon had not expected a lesson in elementary economics. This was ridiculous. But he controlled his impatience, and answered, 'Well, I imagine that it would be the man who had been let off the larger debt.'

'Right,' said the young man. Then he turned to the woman, who was still sitting at his feet, with her head resting on his knee. 'You see this woman?' he said, 'I came at your invitation into your home. You know the way I've been living, that I've done a lot of walking, but you didn't ask me if I'd like a wash. She thought about my sore feet. I came as your guest, but you weren't really interested in me, only in the amusement I might provide for your friends and what I could do for you. Very subtly, you've done everything you could to reinforce the fact that I'm an outsider, a freak, an object for condescension. She gave me a true welcome, because she tried to show that she cared about me, that she was thinking of me, that she wanted to give me something of herself. You've offered nothing of yourself, you haven't reached out in any way to put me at my ease. I'm telling you, she's done a lot of things in her life that she's ashamed of, she's got used to using and being used, she's known the wretchedness and loneliness of hating herself. But the fact that she can still find it within her to do something of beauty and selflessness, that someone who has every reason to despise love because she's experienced its corruption has been able to become vulnerable in a true gesture of love, that proves that she has been enabled to rediscover innocence. The awful burden of a hateful life has been removed, and her thankfulness has just overflowed.

'And you, you're uncomfortable with the overflowing, aren't you? The signs of great love disturb you. And that's because you've never known that kind of liberation. You don't know how good life feels when it's given back to you, because you've never come remotely near losing it. There are deep wounds of pain and shame in her, that every passing encounter, every strange bed, every unfamiliar body drove deeper. But take the guilt and shame away, and the great holes can become filled with love, deep springs welling up and overflowing. But if you don't feel the hurt of your life, if your debt's only a little one, it doesn't make so much difference when it's taken away.'

Then the young man looked straight at the woman, and tenderness was in his eyes. 'You are forgiven,' he said gently.

Simon's face burned. If he was honest with himself, he knew that what the young man had said about him was true. There had been no genuine welcome or reaching-out in his behaviour. Still, he did not like hearing it. He had become used to people who dissembled, who told him what he wanted to hear, who covered up offence because he was a powerful man. Comparison with a whore – that wounded his vanity. And yet, he was conscious of a strange emotion stirring within him. He could not possibly be envious of the woman, could he? The men who had remained at the table, who had been witnesses to the whole extraordinary scene were muttering among themselves, offended. What right did anyone have to talk to them about forgiveness? This was intolerable, bringing this kind of intimacy, of interference into a civilized house. Who was this young man to go forgiving anyone? What gave him the right to judge one of their own? Simon knew that there were men here tonight who would never forget, nor let him forget that they had suffered this outrage.

The young man pulled the woman to her feet. 'You had enough faith to believe it could happen even to you, and it did,' he said. 'May there be peace for you now, and whatever happens to you.' And he pushed her gently towards the door.

When it was all over, and the last of them had gone, laughing or averting their faces, Simon sat down beside the fire, fighting with the feelings inside him. It was as if the whole foundation on which he based his life had been rocked, all his certainty, all his security in the rules of the game, all his cynicism in playing it. He wanted to weep, torn between the desire to look at his life honestly, and the terrible fear of what he would find. And he wanted to weep because he knew that he would never ever forget the look of pure and blinding love on the face of the whore.

* * *

In this story of Jesus being anointed by a prostitute, there is the implication that the hospitality of Simon the Pharisee, though perhaps observing the outward forms, was lacking in a true spirit of welcome and honour. This was given to him by a woman who was an outcast, and whom Simon obviously expected Jesus to revile, as others did. Instead, Jesus used the occasion, which was one likely to have caused great embarrassment and discomfort among others present for its display of emotional extravagance, to teach them about forgiveness. The person who has been forgiven much will love much. That such a woman might be held up as an example of great love must have been offensive to those who believed themselves to be morally superior to a prostitute. For Jesus to then go on to tell the woman her sins were forgiven must have been adding insult to injury to the Pharisees, who believed only God could forgive sins. For them, this was another example of the blasphemous nature of Jesus' claims.

Some questions to help your own imagining of this story:

1 Imagine how you would feel if this scene happened in *your* house?
2 What are the marks of forgiveness? What does it feel like to be forgiven?
3 Do you feel thankfulness towards those who have forgiven you for something? If not, why not?
4 What do you find most difficult to forgive?

A story of another woman touching Jesus, this time in a very different way, is found in Mark 5.25-34. This woman too sought wholeness from Jesus. Imagine this scene – the woman, the crowds, the disciples. Can you imagine it happening to someone you know?

10. Jesus is Anointed at Bethany

'The sweet smell of the perfume filled the whole house.'
JOHN 12.1–8

Six days before the Passover, Jesus went to Bethany, the home of Lazarus, the man he had raised from death. They prepared a dinner for him there, which Martha helped to serve; Lazarus was one of those who were sitting at the table with Jesus. Then Mary took half a litre of a very expensive perfume made of pure nard, poured it on Jesus' feet, and wiped them with her hair. The sweet smell of the perfume filled the whole house. One of Jesus' disciples, Judas Iscariot – the one who was going to betray him – said, 'Why wasn't this perfume sold for three hundred silver coins and the money given to the poor?' He said this, not because he cared about the poor, but because he was a thief. He carried the money bag, and would help himself from it.

But Jesus said, 'Leave her alone. Let her keep what she has for the day of my burial. You will always have poor people with you, but you will not always have me.'

He changed my life. And I loved him. So I did what I did. It was very hard for me. But not the hardest thing. That came later.

Why did I love him? There are so many reasons. In the beginning, he was a friend of my brother's, whom I loved, and that was enough to make me warm to him from the start. He came around our house a lot, to rest, to unburden himself, to get away for a little from the demands that so many people made upon him. I think our home was a kind of sanctuary for him, and a reminder of how ordinary and sweet life could be – food gracefully prepared, me and my sister arguing, and talk, late into the night. At first, he was just a very good friend, kind and considerate and funny. Then he became more than a friend. He became the person who showed me so many things about myself – good things and bad things. His ideas made me question everything I had ever known and unthinkingly accepted. His words challenged me, sometimes infuriated me, continually changed me. And I listened, and I listened, and I learned. And in response, I found thoughts and convictions springing up deep within me, strong and sure, thoughts that filled me with excitement, and the desire for expression: so many new ways of thinking about God, so many new ways of seeing people, such hope for stale situations. It was as if a whole new world opened up to me. He helped me to see myself as I could be, and when others were disapproving, and wanted me to do the expected thing, he supported me. So I came to love him.

And I loved him too because of what he did for others. So many people who had been written off, marked 'redundant', given no chance, these he took to himself, opened his life up to them, was tender with them, and asked them to do the impossible – and they did it. Somehow with him people found the faith to believe that God loved them, and that they could be healed – crazy people, sick people, ashamed people, people who were poor and uneducated and convinced of their own uselessness. I tell you, I have seen the scales fall

Jesus is Anointed at Bethany

from the eyes of the blind and the crippled walk. I have seen grown men become like little children, running free from heavy loads, and children sit playing on his knee. I have seen even the dead rise up and walk, the dead whom I loved, but could not restore with my love. And I loved him more.

But there was something else. In the end, more than I loved him for myself, more than I loved him for what he was to others, I came to love him for himself, for what *he* was. I loved him because he was a man like other men, and, in the midst of his power, walked the earth in weakness. I loved him for the size of him and the sight of him and the particular way he held his head, and the sound of his voice, and all the things about him that were man, and that were this particular man. And as I watched him with the concentration with which we are conscious of those we love, I realized something. I realized that he carried his humanity, his manhood, as a heavy burden. Oh, not that he was not often lighthearted, and full of delight in life, not that he did not enjoy and seem at ease in the company of men and women and children, not that there was anything brooding or reserved about him. It was simply as if he knew that his humanity, the particular way of being that was his, was going to bring him, and others, pain and sorrow. And this knowledge lay across his back like a great piece of wood. I have seen him just once bowed under it, and it touched me more deeply than I could have imagined. But I think I shall live to see him bowed once again. My sister is convinced that he is the Messiah, the Son of God. I do not know about that, but if it is really true that God is a loving God, as he says, then I begin to glimpse the extent of that love. It could only be a great love which could make the wearing of one's humanity so light and yet so heavy.

When I first knew that I loved him, I was so happy. And for a little while, I had dreams. . . It was a very little while. I dreamed the way people do when they fall in love, of promises of undying devotion, of a secret world of happiness, of marriage and a home and children. I loved him, and I thought he loved me. This is the way of the world when a man and woman love each other. This is what is natural. Oh, my dreams were beautiful! But they were only dreams. Slowly, I came to understand that this was different. Something about the humanity of him which I loved so much made the life of work and marriage and children which is so ordinary, so commonplace, and yet so blessedly comforting and transforming, not a possibility for him.

I could not quite explain it to myself. In part, it was the fact that there should be no limitations on his love. Quite simply, there were too many people who needed him to be the way he was, too many people who had been shut out of intimacy, and wanted to hear that this time there were no limits, no 'this far and no further'. And he did have such an extraordinary way of making himself available, changing plans, interrupting what he was doing as if time had simply ceased to exist, a way which would have been intolerable in a relationship which by its nature demands mutual accountability. He needed to have to be accountable to no one but God.

But I think there was also the need for him to be faithful in carrying the burden of his humanity alone. Not for him the deep solace of flesh upon flesh, the refreshment of spirit given by the one who understands you and absolves you, the singular delight of creation in parenthood, the peace of the marriage bed after all the battles are over for the day. Not for him the holiness, the wholeness of two becoming one flesh. It was almost as if he needed to remain wounded, torn apart, so that all the other broken people, seeing him carrying the burden of his humanity, could know that they too could carry theirs, and that in some mysterious way, could find it light. I have learned from him that God gives many ways of holiness.

But these were only my thoughts, and it may be that I was very wrong, that there was much about him that I did not understand. We all have to follow our own calling, and that rarely takes us where we want to go. It is only later that we are able to look back and decipher patterns or discern purpose. His calling was taking him somewhere I could not go – and, as it turns out, it was taking me in unaccustomed paths also. But it was hard to die to my dreams, and harder not to be able to share his pain or comfort his sorrow. His joy and delight in living, in God, I did share – we all did, it was so vivid and all-embracing. But with someone you love,

Jesus is Anointed at Bethany

you want to share everything, and he had shared *my* sorrow. I wanted to be the one who understood. Now I can see that would not have been appropriate, because there was so much I did not, and still do not fully comprehend.

That was why I did what I did. To show that I loved him, to make an offering of my love; to show that I understood the limitations on my love and accepted them: to show that I understood the need for him to go on being the man he was, and the purpose behind it. I wanted to do something for the pain that was to come. I thought about it carefully, knowing how open to misinterpretation it would be. I knew that some of his friends would certainly not understand, that they would be shocked, horrified at the shattering of convention. Sometimes they were *so* stupid – I had heard their idiotic questions, their foolish claims, their petty quarrels, and marvelled at his patience with them. Often they seemed to be graceless and full of ingratitude, forgetting so quickly what he had taught them. Sometimes I could not believe how they could not see what was staring them in the face, could not see the truth about him. It almost seemed as if it were so much easier for women to recognize him, and to accept what he was. Perhaps we have less to lose by saying 'yes' to love and tenderness and mercy. We do not have to fear being unmanned. But I did not care what they would think – I did it for him. No, what I feared was his response, that he would think what I did was shameful, that *he* would not understand why I did it. And of course, the very doing of it frightened me. Would I be clumsy, would I embarrass him, or myself? How strange a thing it was, and how strange to break through years of conditioning about what was proper and what was not. When the time came, I shook with nervousness, and could find no voice with which to speak. My senses were heightened by the extremity of what I was doing, and touch, smell, heat and cold, sound and sight, all became acute. And my heart hammered as if it were breaking iron.

But everything was all right.

Then that fool started to go on about the expense, and about giving the money to the poor. Well, I have observed that people who talk about the poor but have no capacity for a gesture of extravagance when the moment calls for it, rarely translate their words into deeds. To be of a generous spirit also requires the knowledge that there are times to celebrate, the need to mark something of importance, or simply to say that we have not lost our ability to make a sign of this one moment, to pour everything into it in a great overflowing of richness. To make a feast when the cupboard is all but empty, to do something of beauty in the midst of ugliness, to do the utterly unexpected, these are ways by which we affirm our humanness and our freedom. We will die if we let our symbols of love become defined by our duty instead of by our soaring vision. And it is the very poor, those who have least, in whom I have most often seen this generosity of spirit, this reckless defiance of their poverty. The mean-spirited, those who will not squander their spirits, don't usually waste their money by giving it to the poor. He didn't, anyway. I think he just couldn't bear to see all that money being literally poured away. Well, it was a *lot* of money. It was from my mother, you see, and I had waited to use it. I knew there would come a time for it.

But my love understood. He told him to leave me alone. And he talked about the day of his death. I knew then that he saw that my offering was for his pain. And I realized, as if I had always known but only then become aware of it, that the pain was greater even than I had imagined, that the weight of his humanity was leading him to death. And then, inside me, I grew angry, and shrieked at God, who could do this to such a man. To this I was giving up my love. I could not conceive of such agony.

But in the little time since then, and as I see his time drawing nearer and nearer, and the drama and the fury unfold, my anger has drifted away. I know now that it was necessary for me to release him even to death. It was necessary for me to anticipate his burial, to prepare him for it. No other letting-go goes far enough. I could not hold him back from death. It is the fulfilment of all he is. And so I had to give him to it. As long as I, as long as all of us, refused to face that ultimate separation, as long as we tried to hold him back, to possess him, then he could not be bound by us, because our will for him was not his. He would not be free then, and it is the burden of his humanity to be utterly free, and yet to give himself completely.

Jesus is Anointed at Bethany

I find it a terrible irony that I, who had so many dreams of intimacy, should have ended by performing a rite of a very different kind of intimacy. There must be few women who have prepared the man they love for his death. And yet, this was my calling, to do this for him, and I do not reject it. Perhaps it was easier for me to do – after all, I was not his mother, I only loved him as a man, not as the flesh torn from my body. She is waiting, as I do, in dread, with pride, with such sorrow. But I wait also in confidence. I *know*, with every fibre of my being, having given him over to death because he must be free, as a free man he will be returned to us. Because he loves us. And death itself will not separate us from that love. I do not know how it will be so, only that it will.

Perhaps it is meant to be that way for all of us. Perhaps we must all look forward to the death of those we love, and accept it. Only then will our love be free from fear, only then will we be able to give ourselves unreservedly. Perhaps it is that kind of faith he sought in all of us, to place our lives, and our deaths, in the hands of God and live without limits. I don't know, and it is hard to make sense of it all. There is still so much to be revealed.

In the meantime, I wait, and I wonder, and I think of my love. And when he seems so far away, and when I ache for his suffering, I try to remember what I did, to recapture again my gesture of love. And, when memory is clouded, as sometimes happens, there is a sure way I have discovered of clearing it, one thing which, in the way that a sight or sound or object can, brings it back to me as if it were happening now, this moment. I simply close my eyes, and breathe a deep breath, and I am there again, where the sweet smell of the perfume filled the whole house...

* * *

This is another story of Jesus being anointed by a woman, this time Mary of Bethany, sister of Martha and Lazarus. Though there are some similarities to the story in Luke's Gospel, there are also some important differences. In Luke's account, the woman was an unnamed prostitute, despised and sinful, and Jesus uses that incident to teach about forgiveness. In John's Gospel, the occasion and the person are both very different. The occasion happens shortly before the crucifixion, and is seen as being a preparation for death. The person is a respected member of the community, with her brother and sister a close friend of Jesus. Her house is a place where Jesus went to rest and relax. Mary is one of a very few people in the Gospels whom Jesus is described as having loved. Their relationship was obviously a deep one.

For Mary to do what she did must have been at tremendous cost. It was considered shameful for a Jewish woman to appear in the presence of male guests with unbound hair, it had scandalous sexual connotations, and could bring embarrassment upon her family. But for Mary, love was stronger than convention.

Some questions to help your own imagining of this story:

1 What images (pictures, sounds, smells) come to you when reading the story?
2 Have you ever seen someone do something very unconventional for someone they love?
3 Have you ever done something very costly for love?
4 What could you do to prepare someone you love for death?

In this story, we see that Mary has recognized in Jesus someone very special, someone who brought something new into her life. Another story which describes how some people encountered Jesus, first of all failed to recognize him, but finally realized who and what he was, is the passage in Luke 24.13-35, about the walk on the road to Emmaus. You might like to imagine that you are walking on the road to somewhere near your home town, when a stranger joins you, and starts to ask you what you are talking about. How do you answer him?

APPENDIX

Imagining the Gospels as a Group Activity

It can be very rewarding to imagine stories from the Gospels in a group, and to share the fruits of that. We learn from one another's insights, and our own understanding increases when we try to formulate it for others. A group should do this in the way that seems most appropriate for them, but if this is a new idea, you might like to try the following suggestions.

Have the group sit in a circle, or round a table, where they can see each other face to face. Read the chosen passage through first, either with one person reading it, or with the whole group reading a verse or two each in turn.

Then try to get a feeling for the story by sharing a little about how you each see it. You might begin by asking a question that's quite easy for everyone to answer without feeling uncomfortable, such as 'What's one thing that strikes you about this story?' It is good to get everyone in the group to answer the first question, even if it is only a sentence, because then they have at least heard the sound of their own voice to give them more confidence.

You might move on to talk about how the story makes you feel, and then how you understand or interpret the story, and finally, what the story makes you want to do. Just let people answer this as they feel comfortable. It's important that the group respects each other's thoughts and feelings. People may be very tentative or unsure of their answers, and there's nothing more guaranteed to make someone feel completely inadequate and to destroy the power of imagination in them than to have another in the group collapse in uncontrollable laughter, exclaiming 'I never heard anything more ridiculous in my life!', or 'what rubbish! Jesus couldn't possibly have meant that!' This activity is to help people use their imagination in meeting Jesus in the story, not to lecture them on anyone's idea of doctrine.

At this initial stage of discussing the story, it might be

helpful to have a good basic commentary on the Gospels available (suggestions of a couple are given at the end of this appendix). This will allow you to get a feel for the historical context for the story, so that you are clear, not just about its background but about its purpose. Things that we sometimes assume about Gospel stories may have had a quite different meaning in Jesus' time, and this may change the meaning of the stories.

Then ask the group to imagine this story taking place now. You can either discuss and agree on a common setting for this (e.g. you might say 'let's imagine this happening in our local church') or you can leave members of the group to choose their own setting. You can then either allow this group to imagine the story individually, and then share their imagining with the rest, or you can build up a picture together (e.g. . . . and what do we imagine happened next?). If the group is being asked to identify with one of the characters in the story, it is important that they choose this themselves, and that it be a character they feel comfortable with. This is not a role play, where people are being asked to take a part they don't necessarily feel in sympathy with, or may find difficult or distressing to play. Imagining the Gospels should begin where *we* are.

Background Reading

The following commentaries are straightforward and clear: *One-Volume Bible Commentary* by William Neil (Hodder & Stoughton), the *Daily Study Bible* series by William Barclay (The Saint Andrew Press), and the *Torch Bible Paperbacks* published by SCM. *Jesus Christ: His Life and His Church* by Margaret Baxter is a good introduction to the New Testament books and the early Church (SPCK). You might also find two books in the 'Knowing Christianity' series useful: *The Life and Teaching of Jesus* by William Neil and (if you are planning to use Old Testament passages) *The Old Testament* by Robert Davidson (both Hodder & Stoughton).